Now
What Do I Say?

Practical Workplace Advice for Younger Women

Now What Do I Say?

Practical Workplace Advice for Younger Women

Anne Krook

Text copyright © 2014 Anne K. Krook
All Rights Reserved
ISBN 978-0-692-35326-4

In memoriam
Marilyn Sibley Fries
1945–1995

Contents

Acknowledgments   ix
What Is This Book About, and Who Is It For?   1
Now What Do I Say?   7
  WHETHER, WHEN, AND HOW TO ENGAGE   10
    Whether to engage   11
    When to engage   13
    How to engage   14
  INTERACTIONS   19
    You, an individual   19
      You don't exist   19
      You do exist, but you're not really good   23
      You might be good, but your work doesn't matter   30
      You exist as a body   33
      Physical presence and physical contact   43
    Your job   48
      Your job is whatever I need you to do for me   48
      It's nobody's job, and therefore it's yours   50
    You and I   52
      What you heard is not what I meant   52
      What you heard is not what I said   54
      You don't know what to say   56
      No   58
      E-mail and texts   61
      Talking to your boss   62

CONTENTS

    Inside the workplace   64
        Office décor   64
        Office social events   66
        Vendor demonstrations   68
        Interviews   70
        Requests for donations   72
        When people leave   74
        Small workplaces   77
    Outside the workplace   79
        Trade shows and other business events   79
        Recruiting events   82
        Client demonstrations   83
  WHEN IT DOESN'T WORK   85
  WHAT NOT TO ACCEPT   86
  WHEN TO LEAVE   90

Planning Ahead   93
  FOCUS ON YOUR COMPANY AND YOUR AUDIENCE WITHIN IT   95
  FOCUS ON YOURSELF   99
  TEN WORKPLACE COMMANDMENTS   103

Life Outside Of Work   111
  FINANCES   111
  HEALTH INSURANCE   113
  SOCIAL MEDIA   115
  IF YOU HAVE KIDS   116
  IF YOU DON'T HAVE KIDS, BUT YOU MIGHT HAVE KIDS   117

Why Do We Still Need This Book?   121
  A SPECIAL NOTE FOR MEN   124
  A SPECIAL NOTE FOR MORE SENIOR WOMEN   125

Feedback   129

Acknowledgments

WRITING THESE ACKNOWLEDGMENTS has reminded me how much help I have had over the years, in advice and counsel and in role models.

First among many are my parents, **Nancy and Lennart Krook**. In graduate school, when I got a notice from the IRS claiming I owed them what was a lot of money for a student, I grumbled but was going to pay. My mother reviewed the notice and said "Nonsense. You were right, and you're going to appeal this and win." She was right, and I did, and I did, but looking back her initial reaction was what mattered most. My father taught many graduate students in veterinary pathology, and thought and often said, to me and to many, that the best one he ever had was a woman, and he supported her career and the careers of other women consistently. He also voted for on-site daycare at his workplace long before that issue got much sympathy from other senior male faculty members. They both walked the feminist walk as I grew up, and I am grateful.

Mary Ann Nevins Radzinowicz, my dissertation director, embodied and set high scholarly standards. Heaven knows I needed that and valued it, but she also did something I have come to value even more: she was a model of intellectual openness, supervising many students who didn't share her approaches but whom she supported anyway. **Abigail J. Stewart** was an inspiring, collegial presence at the University of Michigan and has remained a trusted advisor and friend since then. She said "[i]t makes all the sense in the world" when I asked her about this book, and I am particularly grateful for that initial support. **Michelle Wilson** had an endlessly demanding senior corporate job and still made time to advise me at crucial moments over several years. **Julie Benezet** has been a source of calm, practical professional guidance and excellent red wine for two decades.

Every single person who discussed or read early versions of this manuscript made it better. Thanks to James Austin V, Julie Benezet, Liz Birkholz, Casey Ellsworth, Kevin Engelbart, Juliet Feibel, Kasz Maciag, Amy Morgans, Connie Palmore, Abigail J. Stewart, and Mary Jo Stojak for reading and commenting on various stages of the manuscript. Particular thanks go to Kasz Maciag, who lived with the book and with me while I wrote, and gave it a focused, thorough, helpful review.

It's my pleasure to acknowledge the professionals who made a manuscript into a book. **Rebecca Staffel** edited it and made it immensely better, and also gave me the benefit of her years of experience in publishing and the depth of her tact ("You do have a few verbal tics"). **Beth Potts** line-edited and copyedited the text with the subject-matter expertise, precision, and attention to detail I used to take for granted from her but don't any more. Cover designer **Jane Jeszeck** was patient with the book and with me and iterated designs fast and well. Book designer and ebook formatter **Susan Gerber** also iterated designs quickly and showed me how much clearer her work made my text. Despite all their excellent work, there are still errors, and all those are mine.

Now What Do I Say?

Practical Workplace Advice for Younger Women

What Is This Book About, and Who Is It For?

NOT LONG AGO, a group of younger women came to me for advice about some trouble they were having in their workplace. A couple members of their team assumed they were all group assistants (an odd assumption, since there were none at that company) and asked them to do administrative tasks they did not ask their male colleagues to do. One or two other members of their team knew they weren't assistants, but asked them to do those administrative tasks for them anyway.

These women faced a common dilemma: like all good employees, they wanted to make sure the work got done, and they also wanted to be respected and treated like everyone else, but they didn't know what answers would help them accomplish both of those goals. Sometimes, by the time they figured out what to say, the right moment to say it had passed, and the missed opportunity exasperated them. Sometimes it was enough extra effort to engage with those remarks that they let them go, and then they felt guilty about not engaging. They were frustrated, not only with their colleagues' behavior but also with their own: by not having responses at hand, they felt they were allowing the behavior to continue. At the very least, they felt they had not done anything to try to stop it.

They came to talk to me, I later found out, for several reasons. I had a reputation for listening to younger women, and for taking their concerns about their workplace seriously. They knew I had had a variety of jobs in a variety of companies, from very large to mid-sized to tiny startup companies. They also were aware I had worked outside the corporate world, as a university professor and as a bartender, and that I served on the board of directors of a national nonprofit organization. Finally, they had heard that, when a problem arose for one of my teams, I had found something relevant for the group to read, got everyone a copy, and discussed it with them as part of solving the problem. In short, they expected that I would listen, have some advice for them, and provide guidance for follow-up.

We discussed their situation, and I gave them some advice about what to say, to whom, and when. Afterwards I went looking for something for them to read: blogs, websites, Twitter streams, articles, books. I found surprisingly little tactical advice for women in the workplace trenches. There's plenty of excellent material on finding your ideal career, managing your career, and changing careers. There's also excellent advice for women on how to develop into and position themselves as senior leaders, of which Sheryl Sandberg's *Lean In* (Knopf, 2013) and the blog associated with it (www.leanin.org) is the best-known recent example. What I didn't find was much material that gave advice about what to do in the following situations, and others like them:

- A colleague asks you to order sandwiches for a meeting you aren't attending when that isn't part of your usual job.
- A colleague walks by your cubicle after a contentious meeting where the two of you have publicly disagreed and mumbles "Bitch!" loud enough for you to hear.
- A vendor, or sales representative, or supplier calls or comes by, and, when you ask about the product line, asks to see "the person I can talk to," incorrectly assuming that person is not you.

WHAT IS THIS BOOK ABOUT, AND WHO IS IT FOR?

These kinds of interactions are common. Many younger women report routine interactions at work that, intentionally or unintentionally, question their authority, their competence, and their intelligence.[1] They report the strain those interactions put on them at work, and how that strain often extends into their home life. Above all, they want to know what they can do about it. I wrote this book to provide guidance for women facing day-to-day situations like these, especially for women in earlier stages of their working lives, to improve their daily interactions at a detailed level.

The bad news is that there are a lot of these sorts of interactions in many workplaces, and at least some of them almost everywhere; the good news is that there is something you can do about it. Most of the situations I discuss are products of ignorance or thoughtlessness, albeit often deeply ingrained and socially supported by both men and women. There are people who have not encountered many women in their workplaces or fields, or they have encountered so few that they are awkward around them in work situations, however well-intentioned they may be. Some people forget what it is like to be early in one's career, without much experience and the confidence that comes from it. And sometimes people have bad days, or a run of bad days, at work or at home, and behave badly as a result. What all that means is that, in many cases, these interactions are addressable: many can be managed by fact-based responses, delivered with varying degrees of patience, persistence, intelligence, and humor. Others, unfortunately, cannot be handled in these ways, and some actually are badly motivated. I discuss tactics for addressing these.

---

1. There are too many distressing examples of younger women being treated poorly in the workplace even to think about giving a comprehensive overview. Here's one example from Silicon Valley: Lauren C. Williams, "Julie Ann Horvath's GitHub Departure Shows Silicon Valley Has More to Learn About Gender Equality," *ThinkProgress*, March 19, 2014, http://thinkprogress.org/economy/2014/03/19/3416013/github-julie-ann-horvath-sexism/.

3

In this book, I discuss interactions younger women often face in their workplaces, provide a range of responses that might be useful in the moment, and give some guidance about when and how to use them and what to do when the responses fail to help. More briefly, I also provide guidance for thinking through, in advance, how to react in support of your longer-term interests in the workplace, including what might help prevent these situations from arising in the first place, to the extent that you can. Finally, a short chapter provides guidelines for the planning that prevents women's home lives from unduly spilling over into their workplaces.

Note that in discussing these interactions, I don't assume the other person is male, though that is often the case. Certainly, it is more often male employees who assume, say, that younger women should perform administrative tasks. It is by no means true, however, that all male employees act that way and that no women employees do. The responses I give will work no matter the gender of the other person. That said, there are some situations that are overwhelmingly gender-specific, and I address those.

While the material in this book is most applicable for women working outside the home, the so-called paycheck workforce, some of it will apply to women in other situations: volunteering on committees in nonprofits, schools, and houses of worship; working on farms; working solo at a home-based business; attending school or some kind of training program. If you're in a working situation not covered here, you want to see your situation covered in more detail, or you have a question specific to your situation, please e-mail me at book-feedback@annekrook.com and ask me to cover it in a future edition. I can't respond individually, owing to the volume of e-mail I get, but I read it all. Needless to say, if I do address your question in a future edition, all individually identifying details will be completely anonymized. I do this not only for everyone's privacy but also because a working lifetime

WHAT IS THIS BOOK ABOUT, AND WHO IS IT FOR?

has taught me that if it is happening to you, it is almost certainly happening to many others as well.

Broader changes that we would all like to see, which create workplaces where these situations do not arise in the first place, are not my main focus. I do believe, though, that the advice here will help women become more comfortable and confident by giving them some responses and options for their daily workplace interactions. The more women are confident and comfortable in their workplaces, the more likely we all are to achieve workplace environments that enable everyone to work productively together. Here, then, are those responses: whether, when, and how to make them, and what they are.

Now What Do I Say?

AT THE HEART OF THIS CHAPTER is a series of verbal interactions women often have with their colleagues. Some of them have happened to me, some to women I know, and some have been reported to me; not one is fictional. All have been made anonymous, as the least significant detail about each incident is the companies where they occurred and the specific individuals involved: these situations, or versions of them, happen in most workplaces with all different kinds of people.

I focus on verbal interactions because they ruthlessly highlight all the differences between a woman early in her career and the person she is engaging with. E-mail or spreadsheets, presentations or drawings, and artwork or code are in some ways more neutral turf, where it is easier to be more disinterested with the individual doing the work.[2] But a younger, shorter, smaller woman reveals herself as such the second she walks though the door into a meeting.

First, some definitions. When I refer to "tactics," I mean both the immediate, short-term responses that you need in the

---

2. For a well-known example of what happens when an artist is thought to be a man and later revealed to be a woman, see Toril Moi, *Sexual/Textual Politics: Feminist Literary Theory* (London: Methuen, 1985), 34–35. For my purposes here, the point is that her work was able to be evaluated as a man's because, as it was in print and the artist had a gender-ambiguous name, her gender was not immediately apparent, something face-to-face interactions don't allow.

moment when these situations arise and the rationales for the quick decisions you make: Ignore this or not? Take it seriously or brush it off with a joke? Address it publicly or privately? You need responses that make the situation better, or at least not worse, right then. When I refer to "strategy," I mean the behaviors and plans that help you achieve the longer-term goals you may have for these interactions: you want to know what type of response helps colleagues change their behavior toward you over time, in case improvement does not happen immediately. You will sometimes find that a tactic helps you in the short term but doesn't serve your longer-term strategic goals. That may be fine: you just have to be deliberate about your choices and realize what the ramifications might be.

In the first part of this chapter I discuss decisions you make as you engage with a colleague, perhaps without your being conscious of them: **Whether, when, and how to engage.** The second part details a range of interactions and potential responses you might give in each case. If you're the kind of person who learns best from first considering general principles and then drawing particular conclusions from them (a deductive learner), read the two main sections in the order they appear: **Whether, when, and how to engage** first, and then **Interactions**. If you're the kind of person who learns best from a range of individual examples and then draws general conclusions from them (an inductive learner), read the sections in reverse order: **Interactions** first, then **Whether, when, and how to engage.** After that, I address situations that are unacceptable, most of which you should not try to handle on your own, and make some suggestions for what to do in those cases. If you are not in a position to avoid unacceptable workplace behavior, I provide guidance on what to do. Finally, the last section addresses the issue of when to leave your current position.

This chapter has several goals. While the main one is to give you tactical responses to some common workplace situations, another is to let you see that these are, in fact, common—they don't happen only to you, or in your company, or in your industry. You will probably recognize many situations that you and your colleagues have faced, and it's important to realize that you're not alone. That realization should also lead you to one of your best resources: colleagues at your workplace and peers outside it. Chances are, if you are experiencing a certain scenario, so are others. You should seek advice from people who are in your shoes, or, even better, who have been in them recently with the same people and have successfully come out the other side.

Another goal is to show you that the things you can do and say to improve these situations tend to fall into patterns, so what works for you in one situation has at least some chance of working in another. An important caveat in that last sentence is "for you." You may read some of my proposed responses and think "That would never work for me" or "That would never work here" or "I hate that" or "Wow, she's nuts." That's because you will find that the response that works for your colleague does not work at all for you, even in a similar situation with the same person, and a response that works well for you does not work at all for a friend at another company. These proposals are not rules; they are suggested tactics for your consideration, adoption, and adaptation.[3]

The responses I discuss here are most often simple, but saying them, and implementing the changes they represent, is not easy. It is wearying to be the one pointing out bad behavior, often meeting resistance, seldom seeing quick changes for your efforts, and even more seldom being thanked. You are directly taking on

---

3. "Improvise, adapt, overcome" is a classic formulation of starting with guidance and training and changing almost any of it as needed for your situation. It's especially common in the US Marine Corps as a reminder that training is only the beginning; it is the deployment of skills in real-life situations that puts training to the test and thereby develops and matures it. Mooselick7, "Problem Solving: Improvise, Adapt, Overcome," *Peak Prosperity's Resilient Life*, February 1, 2011, http://www.peakprosperity.com/blog/improvise-adapt-overcome/52001.

specific instances of ingrained behavior that is often supported, even celebrated, in our culture, and it is tiring. You should cut yourself some slack if you find merely contemplating these responses, never mind actually using them, is hard. It is hard, and sometimes you will choose not to engage in this way. That's fine. Deciding when to engage, which battle to pick and which to let go by, is a skill that improves with observation and practice.

You do have some advantages. None of what I propose here requires a lot of money, like a training course that you or your company has to pay for. The sources I have cited are available free online or, in the case of the books, in inexpensive used copies, in case you want to read further. This advice is not a program that needs to be rolled out to an entire workforce to be effective, though it can be incorporated into such programs or used as standalone training. It is meant for individuals to use and adapt as best suits them and their individual situations.

Finally, everything I suggest here improves with practice. Most of these situations recur, and while you won't have the right response at hand every time, you can improve your odds by practicing, whether in front of a mirror, with your significant other, or with friends and colleagues. You can even develop a better response for those times when you truly don't know what to say, when your jaw drops and you think "did I really just hear that?" And because most of the individual responses I discuss are brief, meant to be employed in short workplace interactions, you can get better fast. You will have a chance to see what works, discard what doesn't, and adapt and use the rest.

WHETHER, WHEN, AND HOW TO ENGAGE

The responses for you to consider in the rest of this chapter fall into these general categories: whether to engage, when to engage, and how to engage.

One way to think through the range of responses at your disposal is to compare them to a formulation from business-continuity planning, which involves advance planning to keep a business running during and after a disaster. The options for addressing risks as you plan for a disaster are to prevent, mitigate, prepare, and accept risks. Almost all business-continuity planning involves a combination of these approaches. While you can't prevent an earthquake from striking your workplace, you can mitigate its effects by, say, bolting bookcases to walls to lessen damage and injury from their falling. You can prepare your employees by educating them about what happens during an earthquake and how to react during it, so they will be less likely to panic. You can also decide to accept some of this risk by not moving your business out of an area in which earthquakes take place, because it's worth it to your company to be in San Diego, San Francisco, Seattle, or somewhere else in a seismic zone.

You have similar choices to make in engaging with your colleagues. Can you prevent some of these remarks? Maybe, over time, with a repeated pattern of responses, especially to the same individual over the same issue. Can you lessen or mitigate the effects of these interactions, on yourself, on your reputation as a colleague, and on your team? Definitely. Can you prepare for some of those effects? Absolutely. Can you decide to accept some of them? Yes, and that is a perfectly reasonable approach at times. The point is that you have more options than you may think.

Whether to engage

I am not advising you routinely to ignore certain colleagues or interactions wholesale (tempting though that may be at times). I am, however, advising you to consider indirectly addressing an interaction by ignoring part of it. You can ignore an offensive remark, for example; it is much harder for someone to repeat an offensive remark than to make it in the first place.[4] A colleague may also be willing to make some remarks assuming they will go unchallenged or unremarked. You can say "Sorry, I missed that; can you repeat it?" "What did you say?" The implicit message in all of these options is that the speaker said something that, on reflection, she or he might choose not to repeat.

A variant on these responses is "I must have misheard; could you say that again?" This version has the disadvantage of putting more of the onus on you: you were the one who misheard. It does, however, have the possible advantage of making your standard the one that was violated and, by implication, making the colleague's remark the thing that needs to be explained and excused.

A third variant ignores the offensive part of an interaction to focus on the actual work-related portion. Let's say someone tosses drawings on the table in front of you and says "So, you asked for the drawings, and here they are!" You say "Thanks. When do you need feedback?" or "Great." By engaging with the work and ignoring the other parts (bad temper, condescension, aggravation at needing you, annoyance at being told to get your input) you implicitly make the case about what you both should be doing.

There will be a lot of interactions that you decide to let go without a response. There are many good reasons why: you're too busy that day with your actual job to educate someone; you're too focused on what you need to do after work; you're tired of engaging with that particular colleague; you're tired. Any of that is okay. You don't need to address every single less-than-perfect interaction at your workplace, and you do not need to feel guilt

---

4. Senator Elizabeth Warren, in an interview with Jon Stewart discusses how she reacts to men and women being treated differently in the United States Senate: "Do you actively battle it, or do you ignore it?" he asked; "When you ignore it, you are actively battling it. . . . You try to get to the things that really matter." Elizabeth Warren, interview with Jon Stewart, *The Daily Show*, Comedy Central, April 22, 2014.

when you don't. You have a job to do, after all, and educating others about appropriate workplace interactions isn't it. What you need to do is make sure that, over time, you interact with your colleagues in a way that presents you as a capable colleague, supports a productive, engaging work environment, and allows both unconstrained discussion and quick recovery when things go wrong between colleagues, as they inevitably will from time to time.

When to engage

You can make headway more quickly with these difficult interactions by addressing them as soon as you realistically can, if not when you're in the middle of them. Ideally this means bringing it to the attention of the speaker the same day. If you let it go longer than the next day at the latest, the speaker may not remember the interaction, and almost certainly cares about it less than you do.

The exception to this general rule is when you need to allow a cool-down period after unusually difficult interactions, for your sake, for the other person's sake, or both. Few people are at their best in a temper, after a long, tense meeting, after a late night getting work done, or after an uncomfortable presentation with a client.

Don't revisit long-ago events when you address current situations. There's a fine line between showing someone how his or her behavior is part of a pattern over time, not just a one-off event, and bringing up an example from so long ago that may not be remembered. What you intend as validation in making your point may feel like piling on to the other party. Always begin with the example immediately at hand. If the speaker denies there's a problem, you can decide whether to bring in other examples. Recognize, though, that it's particularly difficult to bring up previous incidents if you did not object to them at the time.

When figuring out what to say, remember that some of us smolder and some of us burn: some people take in the problem and consider what to say, and others express their discomfort or anger right away. If you tend to step back and think about what to say, and you are dealing with someone who speaks up and speaks out immediately, you may hear something like "If you were uncomfortable, why didn't you speak up then?" A perfectly reasonable response is "I was considering what I wanted to say" or "I wanted to be sure I had all the facts."

How to engage

For the responses I have discussed in the first part of this chapter to work, sort of work, or help make progress, a great deal depends on how you deliver them. The first and strongest influence on how you deliver them is your attitude. You need to start by assuming good intentions. When a colleague says something unexpected or inappropriate, you assume that there is a reasonable explanation: she had a bad day at home, he had a bad day at work, or there is some context that you are not aware of that influences their behavior toward you. You assume until proven otherwise that you have a colleague who generally wants the right thing for the company, for him- or herself, and for you. If you assume good intentions, you will sound as though you do when you address whatever the issue is, and you will get a better response. You will not always be correct in this assumption, and you will find that out fast, but you will get better results if you start from that assumption until you have reason not to.

When you assume good intentions, it is easier to act with professional courtesy. Professional courtesy means that you and your colleague assume some things about each other: you both have something to say, it is worth saying, and the person you disagree with shares these same assumptions. It means that you will use agreed-upon standards of what counts as reasonable, and that changing those standards will happen by discussion and mutual agreement. That's the ideal, and it doesn't always happen in workplaces, but if you assume good intentions from the start, it is much more likely that you will behave with professional courtesy and receive it in turn.

Once you start by assuming good intentions and acting as though you do, two aspects of your delivery influence reception more than any others: a fact-based response, and a neutral affect. The former concerns content, the latter concerns style.

The fact-based response implicitly supports your standing in the discussion. If you are being put down, or your ideas ridiculed or ignored, you respond with facts: "When [this idea] was tried on another occasion, it led to an X% increase in [key metric]." "Our competitor offers this service, and it accounts for X% of their new business in our region." "I am happy to have helped you out last time, but this isn't what I am supposed to be doing; [X] is. The person who can regularly help you do this is [Y]." If the content of your remarks is accurate, complete, and verifiable, it is much harder to dismiss what you are saying. It also allows you to make the interaction about the work, which, in a workplace, it should be. In fact, you can often steer people to a productive discussion by saying "Let's just focus on the topic at hand" or "Let's get back to [topic], okay?" or "We don't have a ton of time right now, so let's get through [topic]."

Neutral affect, on the other hand, is about the style in which you deliver your fact-based response: it means an even tone in which emotion is not a dominant force. I once described this to a colleague as the technique of discussing something problematic or contentious as though you were reading from a laundry list. You wouldn't read from a laundry list with deep personal investment: "Oh, I did have that cleaned two weeks ago; and I need to take four pairs of pants to the cleaners, not three" is about the extent of it.

When you say fact-based things in a neutral way, you achieve several things at once: you are reasonable, you sound reasonable, and you remove or reduce any perceived threat of an emotional response. If the person to whom you are speaking is thinking "Oh, no, she is going to freak out! Or, like, cry!" (whether that has any basis in reality or not), what you say will be less effective than it could be. Neutral affect helps you and the person to whom you are speaking focus on the content of what you are saying. It's a particularly useful tool for women, who are perceived to be much more emotional than men, a trait that, whether accurate in any given individual's case or not, tends to be used against them.

Once you have fact-based responses delivered with a neutral affect, you have achieved a good deal. You are reasonable because you are fact-based, and you sound reasonable because you have expressed yourself with a neutral affect. There are other techniques that you can choose to deploy, but if you adopt only these two, you will help yourself a lot.

Among the other techniques that can also assist in making your point, repetition is the most frequently used. By repetition, I don't mean repeating the same phrase over and over, in the same tone, a surefire way to annoy the person with whom you're speaking. I mean making the same point, over and over, as often as you need to, on separate occasions. You will need some connective phrases to remind your listener: "The point I was making was [point]" "The last time I raised this issue, I argued that [point]." "Tuesday we decided [decision]; do we have reason to change?" It's not that repetition in and of itself is useful, but you want to return again and again to the work and to the kind of personal interactions that stay focused on work rather than on extraneous things.

You may find yourself frustrated when you have to repeat yourself about what seem to be basic workplace courtesies. While you are right to be frustrated, remember also that it takes a long time for some people to learn new ideas, even if that brand-new idea is "I ought not to ignore this person in my next meeting" or "Even if I think she's a bitch, I shouldn't say it." Progress rarely happens all at once, and pointing out the way you prefer to be treated may take time to sink in and even more time to come to influence previous and ongoing social training, such as the kind that tells your colleague that "bitch" is a fine term for intelligent women with opinions.

A variant on repetition is engaging other colleagues who share your point of view, so you are not the only one supporting your point. It is rare that you are the only one having difficult verbal interactions with a particular colleague. Once you know this is the case, and have discussed a particular interaction with others, you can ask for their input: "[Colleague], what do you think?" You can also refer to them indirectly: "At the last meeting, [colleague] also liked that idea." These kinds of indirect mentions that support your point of view can be effective, especially when they reference someone senior, powerful, or respected in your workplace. This approach does, however, carry the risk that you may be perceived as not making the argument purely on your own merits.

Humor is another tactic that you can deploy. It conveys goodwill and approachability, and implicitly makes a commitment to not taking oneself too seriously. It invites the listener to take the side of the speaker, to see things from the same perspective, and laugh. It is above all disarming, potentially taking away some or all of the threat you may represent to the speaker, whether that threat is realistic or not.

Successfully using humor depends in part on your emotional intelligence about yourself and your workplace: you need to understand how your humor will be received.[5] Some caveats matter more than others when it comes to humor. Humor has a strong cultural influence, and what sounds jokey, casual, and funny in one culture or workplace may sound aggressive, rude, and mean in another.[6] As you might expect, there is also a strong language component to humor: if you are telling a joke in your native language, non-native speakers of that language may have a harder time understanding it, particularly over a speakerphone on a conference call. If it is not clear to them that they aren't the butt of the joke, they may be offended. If they don't understand the joke enough to laugh along with everyone else, they may feel excluded. One culture may tolerate obscenity but not profanity in humor, while another culture may be the opposite. Finally, humor has a strong physical component for both speaker and listener, as good raconteurs know: they constantly assess how their audience is receiving their story by their physical, especially facial, cues. Jokes told in meetings can be both hilarious to those in the room and unfunny to those on the other end of the conference call who can't see the person telling the joke.

Attitudes toward humor in the workplace as a tool to engage colleagues tend to be binary: people either find it an effective and helpful tool or unfunny and ineffective, rarely anything in

---

5. A good overview of workplace humor and its uses (and risks) for women is Barbara Mackoff's *What Mona Lisa Knew: a Woman's Guide to Getting Ahead in Business by Lightening Up* (Los Angeles: Lowell House, 1990). It reacts to her perception of an earlier era when women could not have as much of a sense of humor, and certainly could not display it. I don't necessarily agree with her perception, but her general advice is sound and her comments on the dynamics of humor are helpful.
6. For an overview of how different cultures communicate and collaborate when it comes to business, see Richard D. Lewis, *When Cultures Collide, 3rd edition: Leading Across Cultures* (Boston and London: Nicholas Brealey Publishing, 2006) and Richard D. Lewis, *When Teams Collide: Managing the International Team Successfully* (London and Boston: Nicholas Brealey Publishing, 2012). The former provides an overview of communication and negotiation styles; the latter explicitly takes up the issue of humor across cultures.

between. Don't think about humor as a skill that you either have or don't, or as something that must be deployed constantly or never. If you think about it as an option that is more useful at certain times than at others, you will be more comfortable deploying it as you find it helpful.

INTERACTIONS

Whether, when, and how to engage are useful as categories to help you think about your options and choices when you interact with your colleagues. You do not, however, interact with your colleagues in general categories: you interact with them in specific conversations. This section provides guidance on how to react and respond to those interactions.

You, an individual

You don't exist

It's hard to imagine a more basic workplace issue than being ignored. These situations fall into two equally infuriating categories: being ignored while you are present, and being ignored while you are not.

♦ In a meeting, you are passed over by the leader when you want to speak, and then the conversation moves on.

Repeat "excuse me" in a level, neutral tone when the current speaker finishes until you are recognized. Mastering neutral affect, sometimes called the laundry list because you speak as though you were reading from something as neutral as a laundry list, is a critical workplace skill. When you are recognized, begin your comment with the most relevant point or data you have to contribute.

- In the meeting, the leader does not respond to your input, but just moves on to the next person.
- In the meeting, the leader does not respond to your input, but does respond to a colleague who makes the same point you made.

At the next opportunity in the meeting, begin by saying "Here's why I made my point [X]" and follow that with the point you made that was ignored. Then continue by showing why it is relevant to the current discussion. You don't need to do this every time, just often enough that you are not routinely overlooked. If it happens more to you than to others, however, or if it happens often, make sure you speak up when you have a strong, relevant point to make that gets overlooked.

- At the end of a meeting, the leader invites some member of the team to go to lunch afterwards, but not you.

There's a difference between being overlooked and being pointedly excluded. If you were overlooked, you can ask "Mind if I join you?" or "Can we continue the discussion at lunch?" Typically, the leader will look startled and say "Sure!"

If you were pointedly excluded, or think you were, your situation is trickier. You need to decide on the spot if you are comfortable asking to join even if you believe you were deliberately left out. The same phrases work as in the scenario if you were inadvertently left out. If you were deliberately excluded, you should follow up with the leader as soon afterwards as you reasonably can. If you cannot address it quickly, you need to decide whether it is worth bringing up the matter at all. Typically I recommend following up on a matter like this no later than the next day (and the end of the same day is better), if this is someone you see routinely at work. Don't let it wait longer than that; the incident may be forgotten after the end of the next day. Remember that something that is important to you may not matter nearly as much to the person who caused it to happen, so you should raise the issue as promptly as you reasonably can.

You should also consider whether the organizer is inviting the others (but not you) to lunch to make a point to them: they weren't prepared for their part of the meeting, they engaged in a way the organizer didn't like, they didn't respond to a client's question clearly, and so on. If you suspect this the case, by all means, don't ask to join. Don't allow this to be your imagined reason why, though. If you were excluded, you should try to find out the actual reason.

In all of these situations, you can take steps to be more visible and thus harder to overlook accidentally. Sit at the table, if possible, rather than in chairs around the edge of the meeting room, and put your hands on the table rather than in your lap, which will tend to make you lean forward and be more engaged.[7] Sit in the leader's line of sight rather than to his or her side where it is harder to be seen, unless team organization or dynamics require that you sit to the leader's side. Don't work on something else on your laptop or other device during the meeting; engage with the content in front of you. Take notes. Wear dark clothing to help you stand out if your workplace has bland, pale backgrounds.

◆ **A brainstorming session in your group or your field is planned, and you are not invited, though your peers are.**

In these situations, your responses depend on whether you hear about the meeting before or after it happens. If you hear about it beforehand, ask the organizer if you may also attend, and if

---

[7]. There's a discussion of this specific point in *Lean In*: chap, 2, "Sit at the table," 27–38. As the title implies, the entire book addresses women's need to engage more closely and directly with their workplaces.

the organizer hesitates, point out similarly situated peers who were invited. If the organizer responds that the session is full, ask when the next one is, and ask to be invited to that one. You should if possible ask in person, as your e-mail, voicemail, or text may get lost before the session itself takes place.

If you learn of it afterwards, find the organizer, ask when the next session is, and ask to be invited to that one. At that point, the organizer may explain why you weren't invited. If the explanation seems reasonable to you, thank the organizer and ask to be invited to the next relevant session. Find out what key points, discussion, and distributed material you missed. Offer to book a separate time to review the material you missed. At this point, the organizer may understand why you are asking to be invited, or may conclude that it is less trouble to invite you next time than to recount the material and discussion for you.

To find out about these opportunities ahead of time, and therefore to improve your chances of being invited, you should let the organizer and your boss know that you are interested in similar opportunities. You can periodically ask about upcoming ones; put a reminder on your calendar to ask every so often.

♦ **A training session or course is offered to your peers, but not to you.**

This situation depends on whether it is your group offering the training, some other group, or Human Resources (HR). If it is your group or some other group (say you're not in Finance but Finance is offering advanced Excel training that people from many groups attend), the same responses as you use for not being invited to a brainstorming session will work. If it is to HR-sponsored training, ask your HR representative who the training is meant for, and if you are in that group, ask when a session you can attend will be offered.

Some kinds of training involve a smaller group being selected from a larger one: a subset of individuals is selected for management training, or a subset of managers is selected for leadership training to groom them for more senior positions. If you are not selected for this kind of training, sit down with your HR representative or your boss and ask what you can do to be included in the future. Note the difference between asking in that way and asking why you were not included: the former is a positive inquiry and will reflect better on you than the latter. If you ask either question, be prepared for an answer that may require you to make necessary changes in your performance to be included.

One thing you must do: if you are not included in a training session that is relevant to your performance in your current job, it is important to have a record of this. Note when you got the training, or that you didn't, if you don't. When it comes time for performance evaluation, you want your manager to know what training you got when, which will matter if it is different from what your peers got. See "Keep a work diary" in the "Planning ahead" chapter.

You do exist, but you're not really good

This broad category of interactions dismisses your intelligence, your competence, or your authority. They are difficult enough one on one, and they can be even more difficult in front of others. These remarks are often made when you are not present and get back to you, well-intentioned or maliciously, or are said in your earshot (deliberately or not), but not to you directly.

A word of caution: when these remarks are repeated to you, bear in mind that there is at least one person between your hearing it and the person who actually made the remark. It may be that whoever is repeating the remark misheard or has private motives for either repeating a painful remark or editing it in a way that misrepresents the original intention. A suitable response to almost any less-than-complimentary remark passed along to you is "I'm sorry to hear that; I'll listen for it."

Note the difference between remarks used to put others down and appropriate performance evaluation. In a performance evaluation, your manager or someone with responsibility for your work engages directly with your work, your ideas, and your behavior rather than making broadly dismissive comments. Remarks used to put others down, on the other hand, mostly address something other than work performance, often in a way so general as to be unanswerable.

- "Can you believe how dumb she is?"
- "Can you believe how silly [that idea] is?"

If the remark is repeated to you, rather than said directly, you can say "I'm sorry to hear that." If you say it in a composed way, you will not seem devastated. You have a right not to *be* devastated at so broad and dismissive a generalization, but that is a different matter.

Such generalizations have the disadvantage (among many others!) of being unanswerable directly. "I am not dumb" is a losing response in an unwinnable argument: "Yes, you are!" "No, I'm not!" Instead, if you engage the speaker directly, ask specific questions: "What doesn't make sense about [idea]?" Specific questions have specific answers, don't permit broad generalizations as answers, and lead to more productive conversations. A snarkier version is "What about it doesn't make sense to you?" This response implies that whatever you did or said does in fact make sense. Which formulation you use depends on how you inflect your comments along the sarcasm scale and how well you know the speaker. You can use sarcasm directly: "That's helpful," pointing out how unhelpful that kind of remark is, whether or not the speaker had a reasonable point to make about your idea.

In this case, you can also deploy the nearly all-purpose response "Excuse me?" The force of this phrase depends heavily on its inflection: "Excuse me?" in a relatively neutral tone implies you might not have heard, or heard correctly. "ExCUSE me!" more emphatically means you found the speaker's remark offensive or inappropriate enough to call it out publicly. "Excuse ME!" draws enough attention to you to point out to everyone that in fact it is the speaker who needs excusing.

- "She did all right, but she had help."
- "She did all right, but [colleague] did the key stuff."
- "She did all right, but [colleague] really did the work."

The implication here is that you may have done good work, but it isn't really owing to you at all, and by extension you are not really that good at your job. You can say "Of course I had help!" if you did, and "I sure did have help, and [colleague] was great to work with." Very few remarks you make will shut someone up faster than this one, in my experience.

You can say "Yes, [colleague] did [this part] of the analysis, and I did [this other part]." Especially if you are generous with the praise and the credit for the work, you will not seem as though you are claiming credit for someone else's work when you describe what you, in fact, did.

Do not think this is happening to you only because you are young, new to your workplace, or junior in your field. One of the authors of an MIT study about discrimination facing female scientists in the last quarter of the twentieth century noted that "even when women win the Nobel Prize, someone is bound to tell me they did not deserve it, or the discovery was really made by a man, or the important result was made by a man, or the woman really isn't that smart."[8]

The last of the three remarks, "She did all right, but [colleague] really did the work," is potentially serious, if the speaker is accusing you of taking credit for work you did not do. In that case, you describe what you did in as neutral a tone as possible, though it is hard not to be annoyed at remarks like this one. "Actually, I did [parts you did]; [colleague] did [other part]." "Actually" and other terms such as "in fact" are how you start contradicting the speaker; facts are how you finish. If you believe your colleague is serious about the remark and not merely jealous, keep your work notes, especially if you hear of these remarks secondhand.

The ability to acknowledge who did what correctly and completely, and to share credit generously, will take you farther in your career than almost any other trait.

◆ "Get a guy's help with this."

In this case, you may be in the middle of something or encountering a problem, and you are advised explicitly to get help from a male colleague. If there is ambiguity about "guy" in this context, make sure the speaker is not merely advising you to get some help, as opposed to advising you to get specifically a male colleague's help: "I could probably use some help; did you have someone particular in mind? Maybe [talented woman colleague]?"

If the speaker did in fact mean that you should get help from a male colleague, as opposed to a woman, find out if there is a reason for that approach. Relative physical attributes of strength, height, or reach aside, there should not be any reason to get help from a male colleague, rather than a particular individual with

---

8. Nancy Hopkins, quoted in "Can You Spot the Real Outlier?" Eileen Pollack, *New York Times Magazine*, October 6, 2013, 30-35, 44-46.

the skills you need, who may or may not be male. You can use humor: "Yeah, guys are stronger, which really helps with Excel." "Yeah, the tall guys are good with drawings." You can ask, straightforwardly, "Do you mean that I should get a man's help?" Put that way, you might hear something shamefaced in response: "No, I mean, I just thought you needed some help." That has a simple response: "Yes, I do; who is the right person to help me with [problem]?" or "What kind of help would you advise?" Then you can discuss the skill-set or information you need, not the gender of the individual supplying it.[9]

◆ **"She did all right, but she isn't really that smart."**

This is one of the most infuriating remarks you will encounter: it's unanswerable, unverifiable, and irrelevant. Because everyone has things they do better or worse than some other people, a poorly motivated person will be able to find something bad to say about everyone, no matter how smart they are and no matter the quality of their work. This kind of remark is often made as a snide aside, in the expectation that no one will disagree with the speaker, and at the very least no one will answer. If you respond, you may have the advantage of surprising the speaker.

If the remark is made directly to you and about you, which is exceptionally rare, you can say "I guess we'll see how customers like it" or "We'll see what the market thinks." Saying "We'll see what the boss thinks" is riskier in that the speaker is likely to hear it as a more personal challenge rather than an appeal to what customers think. Focusing in this way on the irrelevance of the

---

9. For a hilarious example of this comment, see Fredrik Gertten, "The Invisible Bicycle Helmet," Focus Forward Films. Swedish with English subtitles: http://vimeo.com/43038579. Two women industrial design students, raising money for a bicycle helmet that inflates when needed, are advised by an older male venture capitalist, with reference to female managers, "Get a rooster, and there will be order!" You can't make this stuff up.

remark has a couple of advantages: it makes the speaker's standard seem silly in the face of actual customers and actual success, and it focuses on the work itself.

If such a remark is made about someone else in your earshot, you can say "The project seems to have gone fine" or "The customer was really happy" or "I heard her boss loved it." Depending on how well you know the speaker, you can say "Anxious much?" or a more nuanced "Her work is great; why do you think she isn't smart?" or "Her work is really great; what don't you like about it?" or "She's a great colleague, and I'd work with her any time."

♦ **"She didn't attend [currently prominent school your field], after all."**

This kind of remark can be used no matter what your educational background actually is, as long as it differs from the speaker's current ideal or the speaker's own. As a result, this kind of put-down is unanswerable; the trick is showing that it is also irrelevant. This put-down anchors itself firmly in the now-unchangeable past, so that, in the speaker's mind, there is nothing the subject of the remark can do about it. On the contrary, there is everything you can do about this kind of remark: you can make it irrelevant. The one-word response in the moment is "True." This kind of comment will vanish more quickly than any other, as results at work rapidly overshadow educational achievements.

One trick that may help: look up every executive or senior leader at your company on LinkedIn or in company bios, if your company has them, and find out where they went to school or did their training. If you are at a medium-sized or larger company, odds are that at least one of them attended an institution or program just like yours. I was once on a conference call for a hiring meeting, and as part of his critique, a colleague mentioned that the candidate had not gone to a selective college. I mentioned the college where our CFO, widely acknowledged to be a brilliant woman, had gone, rightly estimating that it would not meet the speaker's definition of selective. I never heard a similar remark from that individual again.

◆ **"She doesn't have a degree in/experience in/come from a company that did [what your workplace does]."**

This remark slights those who have come to their current job in a non-traditional way: a farmer from the city, someone who learned their current skills on the job, someone in a role new to them. Women, in particular women entering the workplace after an absence, often find themselves in this position. Two responses help here. To the speaker, you can say "I guess my/her work will have to speak for itself" or "She did well, so so what?" The latter is more aggressive, so expect a response about how much a standard background matters.

The other approach is indirect: if you have a non-standard background, seek out your boss's advice, as well as that of respected colleagues and HR, about ongoing training, inside our outside the workplace. The further along in your career that you are, and the longer you have been in a particular job or role, the less these kinds of comments will matter. What will matter over time is the quality of your work, and you can support that effort by seeking out training.

◆ **"I can't understand why they made her manager of that group."**

If this is said about you and repeated back to you, "I guess I'll just have to demonstrate why with my work" is a useful response.

Resist the temptation to ask who said it. You may also decide not to engage the person who originally made the remark, with one exception. If your current boss is supposed to have said it—assuming he or she isn't the one who made you manager in the first place and presumably knows why you got that role—and if the report came from someone credible, then at your next individual meeting with your boss, you can say "I heard a remark that suggested you were concerned about my management skills; is that correct? If it is, I want to address any concerns you have." Notice that this line gives your boss a chance to say that whoever repeated the remark to you was wrong, or misheard, or misunderstood.

- "Who can I speak to about this?" (When you or someone has made clear that person is you.)
- Variant: "Can I speak to someone in charge?"
- Variant to young-looking women: "Can I speak to the man in charge, missy?"

Patient repetition of facts can be your first response: "I am the person who makes that purchase decision." "I'll be the person taking this report from you today." Since facts don't always deter the person from seeking someone else, you need to be prepared for that person to go to your boss, or your boss's boss, or his close friend at the company. It's critical here for you to have all the data you need (can you in fact get this person everything he needs?), to be factually correct, and, if you think the speaker might go to your boss, let your boss know ahead of time. Make sure your boss knows why you made the decision that made the speaker unhappy.

You might be good, but your work doesn't matter
This category of interactions surfaces when you have done good work, especially work that is acknowledged to be good, and the

person who makes the remarks is threatened by the work, the praise it received, or the funding you got to get it done.

- "Yeah, it came out fine, but it wasn't as important as [other project]."

As with criticism of where you went to school or got your training, these remarks are often unanswerable, because there is almost always some project, somewhere, that is more important than whatever you have just accomplished. You can decide not to address the personal comment at all: "Yeah, [other project] is key" or "I am so glad [other project] came out well." You can respond neutrally: "Everything matters!" You can focus on your customers: "I guess it matters to [customer who paid for it]."

Another option is for you to engage the substance of the criticism. This category of response is most likely to lead to a long back-and-forth, so be prepared for that. "Here's why this project matters: [data, preferably about customers or your product line]." If you get into comparisons, be prepared to compare the projects directly: "This project got [X] done with [Y] resources" or "The return so far is [this]." If you make a good point, be prepared to hear "Yeah, but [this other thing] didn't go as well."

At some point, however good your data or your performance, you will be challenged with an aspect of your work that didn't go as well as the same aspect of another project, however irrelevant. At that point, you may respond with "You're right; [that other team/colleague] did an amazing job."

Depending on how well you know the speaker, and whether there is obvious anxiety about the speaker's work being compared to your own, you can say "Anxious much?" Be prepared for the speaker lashing out, especially if you make this or similar remarks in front of other people. In my experience, this kind of remark is often most effective when it is made in defense of someone else who is not present: "Anxious much? She did great work, and we're lucky to have her." It's hard for the speaker to disagree with that.

- "Women are good at that stuff."

This pernicious remark devalues what you did by saying that women are good at it no matter what; as you are a woman, it is not surprising you would succeed at it. It also devalues your success by implicitly contrasting it with what men are good at. When you hear this, you can say "Really, [male colleague] is great at it, too." Or, less strategically helpful, "[Female colleague] is not actually all that great at it," or "Actually, successful *people* succeed at that stuff."

You can also address the underlying assumption directly: "Do you think there's stuff that only men or only women are good at?" More directly still, you can ask "Do you think there's stuff only men are good at?" You will likely get one of two kinds of response: an embarrassed "not really," in which case you can use the all-purpose neutral remark "oh" or "so . . . ?" and let the question drop, if you want. Or you will hear a defensive or self-assured "Yes, of course!" You can let silence be your answer, or you can say "wow," and let your tone be your answer. Or you can get into it with your colleague in detail, and have him or her describe what kinds of things men are better at than women. It depends on how much time you have and whether you are actually curious about what your colleague thinks about the topic.

- "She *would* be good at that; Asians usually can do math."

This offensive variant of "women are good at that stuff" is one of many remarks that can be generalized to "[Group] is good at [stereotypical skill]." In this case, the remark plays to the stereotype of the Asian success at technical work. The same responses you use for "women are good at that stuff" work in this case. If it is said about someone else in your earshot, you can say "She's not good at that because she's Asian; she's good at that because she's good at it and works hard at it, and we're lucky to have her."

Sometimes when you hear these remarks, it is tempting to cite counterexamples: "I knew an Asian guy who was no good at math at all," for instance. In general you should avoid this tactic for two reasons. The first is that you don't want to get into an argument where every instance of knowing someone with a certain trait counts equally in the discussion. The problem here isn't that some Asians aren't good at math, it's that judging people by stereotypes, and devaluing someone's work because they can be expected to be good at it according to a stereotype, is offensive and incorrect. The second is that you want to focus on the person's positive contributions in the workplace, and engagement in a conversation about the validity of the stereotypes takes away from that focus.

You exist as a body

Most women are all too aware of this category of workplace interaction, which treats women's bodies as appropriate subjects for remarks, commentary, humor, and insult. There's a difference between normal social interaction and comments designed as put-downs or as differentiators between women and men. "Nice jacket!" said between people who are friends outside work means "Nice jacket!" "Nice jacket!" said after a tough presentation may mean "Nice jacket!" but it is not the place to say it, and it may also mean "I was too distracted or immature to pay attention!" It may also mean "I want to talk to you about the content of your presentation, but I can't figure out how, and I need to say something."

Sometimes you'll hear "He can be kind of a jerk to the women, but he says stuff to the guys, too." This statement can be both true and irrelevant: if he makes remarks to you or other women that are inappropriate, his equal-opportunity inappropriateness excuses nothing. Here's a quick test for the relevance of that statement: are the remarks to male colleagues made as put-downs, or are they acknowledgements of social equality? Another is this: does he say them to his respected male peers and those people senior to him in the organization, or only to more junior people? You can say "It doesn't sound to me like he's putting the guys down" or "He doesn't talk like that around [senior figure]" or "He doesn't say that around the guys."

Sometimes you'll hear "Look at his age/his field," which implies and is occasionally explicitly followed by "Everybody his age/in his field acts like that, and some are way worse." This comment is both insulting and incorrect. You can say "[Other colleague his age/in his field] doesn't say stuff like that" or "Others may be worse, but what he said was bad enough." You can add "I don't care" if you want to bring yourself as a standard into the discussion: "I don't care if others are worse, what he said was bad enough." "I don't care if others are worse; he's the guy who said that." I recommend starting without "I don't care" phrases, emphasizing what the other person said rather than focusing on what you find it offensive.

◆ The term "girl": "You should ask the other girls how to do that."

Whether or not this term is inappropriate depends on many things. Incredible as it may seem, there are some workplaces where the standard term for male employees is "boys," in which case "girls" as its counterpart is not as bad. The difficulty, of course, is that "girls" is more condescending to women than "boys" is to men. In such a workplace context, however, it is harder to object than it is when the counterpart is "guys" or "men."

If the routine counterpart for "girls" is "guys," you have more options for your response. In more and more workplace contexts, "guys" is a gender-neutral plural. If that is true of your workplace, you can say "Don't worry, you can include me with the term 'guys'" or "'Guys' works for me, too."

The difficulty is when the routine terms used are "men" and "girls," a clear status difference. In that case, depending on how well you know the speaker, you can say "Oh, you can refer to us all as 'guys.'" Bear in mind that the older the speaker, the less likely he or she is to be comfortable with that. Another option that sometimes works in this case is feigned surprise: "Girl? I haven't been called that in years." The closer the speaker is to your own age and workplace status, the better this works. If someone responds with either faux or unfeigned gallantry, saying "You're young enough to be called a girl!" you can answer "Thank you, but I am old enough to have to pay the bills!" Depending on the age and perceived good intentions of the speaker, you can choose to leave off "thank you."

The term "girl" is worse when applied to women of color. If this term is directed to or about you in the workplace, you need to address the issue with the speaker as soon as you reasonably can, especially if your boss is the one who uses the term. If you are in a company with an HR staff member or department, make sure you review the circumstances with them as well; HR staff should be clear with the speaker about why this term is not acceptable. In workplaces where you do not have HR resources and you need to address the speaker on your own, you should skip the humor: "Please don't refer to me as a 'girl.'" If the speaker responds with "I didn't mean anything by it" or some similar comment, you can repeat yourself: "I understand; please don't use that term for me."

If the speaker responds with "I don't see what's wrong with it; I call [other woman] 'girl' too," you can say "I can't speak for her, but please don't use that term for me."

- "I like it when girls in the office wear skirts."
- "A lot of girls in the office are wearing short/tight skirts these days. It's unprofessional."

Reponses to this kind of remark depend on your workplace dress code and whether you engage with the term "girls" or "skirts." If it is a formal business environment, where suits and ties for men and skirts and jackets for women are de rigueur, the speaker may be indirectly telling you to adopt the common office dress standard. If you are adopting the standard, or if that is not the standard at your workplace, you can use the all-purpose remark that also means you are not going to engage with that kind of comment: "really?" or "oh." If you have any reason to believe the comment may be well-meant if clumsy advice to change your style of dress, check with a longer-tenured or more senior woman colleague, if there is one, to find out whether this colleague has a history of such remarks to women or if you are, or are perceived to be, out of step with common office dress.

- "Hey, skinny!"
- "Were you always, like, tall?"

If these remarks are meant as an awkward compliment from someone who doesn't actually know what to say, an all-purpose greeting or the simplest answer works: "Hey!" or "Yes!" If they are simply a thoughtless opener to a conversation, the same remarks work, with a bit less enthusiasm: "Hey." or "Yes." Unless you know the speaker well, resist the temptation to answer with snark: "Hey, chubby!" or "Were you always bald?" The path to mutual insults escalates quickly and rarely ends well in the workplace, except among the closest friends and colleagues. Engaging in this way may also give the impression that you believe personal comments like these are fair game in the workplace, which might end well now but not later. In addition, colleagues who overhear it without the context of how well you know the speaker may think twice about your judgment. Be careful when engaging in this kind of back-and-forth.

- "This is the breast hack ever."[10]
- "It's called 'Project Topless.'"

Breast jokes and references are among the more common ways of putting down work done by women, or putting down women themselves by reducing them to a body part.

If a joke or remark like this is made in your presence, you can say "What did you say?" When the person you are talking to repeats the remark, you can answer "*What* did you say?" at which point he might mumble "Nothing." If he giggles or smirks and doesn't answer, you can say, "Don't use that term to describe me/my project." If he responds "Why not? It's funny," you can say "It's not appropriate for a colleague or a project."

I don't recommend the response "I don't find it funny" for two reasons. It leads to an endless, childish cycle of "I think it's funny" and "Well, I don't." The main reason, though, is that it doesn't matter if the speaker does find it funny: that standard isn't appropriate for the workplace.

If remarks like these are directed at you or your work, in addition to responding to them, you should let your boss know. If your boss is making them, you should talk to your HR representative,

---

10. Claire Cain Miller, "Tech's Man Problem," *New York Times, Sunday Business*, April 6, 2014, 1, 4–5. The article discusses the problem of "programmer" culture in technology and breast jokes as one of many manifestations of it.

if you have one, or the most senior person at your workplace whom you trust if you have no HR staff. If you are in a very small workplace and your boss is making these kinds of remarks, you may want to consider revising your résumé and starting to search for another job.

- "Hi, squeaky!" (Said before a meeting where you are presenting. I am not making this up, I swear.)
- Alternatively, comments that you have a high-pitched or otherwise annoying-to-the-speaker voice.

Few things irritate women in the workplace more than comments about their speaking voices, and for good reason. Except for some presentational techniques I note below, it's hard to change the voice you were born with and grew into. And often these kinds of remarks represent indirect or implicit criticism: for whatever reason, the content of your presentation itself is not questioned (or not at this moment), but the quality of your voice is.

In the first case, your answer can be a completely neutral greeting: "Hi," simply ignoring the insulting term. In the second case, the all-purpose neutral reception works: "Really?" "Oh." Depending on how well you know the speaker, you can use humor: "I had NO IDEA my voice sounded like that!" More pointedly, "I have NO IDEA what my own voice sounds like!" You can also lean over to them and say the same thing in a stage whisper. You may hear a defensive "Hey, some people don't!" In that case, you can follow up later with the speaker and explain that you'd prefer to have discussions about your presentational techniques in private. Be careful to distinguish between your presentational techniques and your material itself. If your colleague has comments about the content of your presentation, and used comments about your voice as an opening he was too awkward to make otherwise, engage with those openly and directly, without the sarcasm.

It is infuriating to watch people in a meeting or presentation giggling at your speaking voice. In my experience, nothing other than a neutral response and first-class work improves this situation over time.

- "Bitch."
- "Don't be such a bitch about it."

This term is the all-purpose put-down for strong women, especially when they are right, talented, or somehow threatening to the speaker. It is comparatively rare (though not actually rare, unfortunately) for a speaker to use this term directly to someone's face; it is more common to refer to someone in the third person in this way ("Don't worry about what that bitch thinks").

If remarks like these are made to you, be clear with the speaker about what is appropriate and acceptable: "Don't call me that." "Don't call me 'bitch.'" "Don't use that term for me." I recommend you start with these responses and place responsibility squarely on the speaker to amend his or her language, rather than saying "I find that term offensive." I prefer the former because of its implicit insistence that you not be called a bitch because the term itself is wrong, not because you happen to object to it. I also caution you against apologizing, even rhetorically: "Don't use that term for me" rather than "I'm sorry, but please don't use that term for me." Don't threaten the speaker with HR, your boss, his or her boss, or the company code of conduct: the term just unacceptable. Of course, whether you do raise the matter with HR, your boss, or the speaker's boss is a different issue.

Sometimes you will hear "Hey, I mean that as a compliment." You can say "I don't hear you saying it to men," or "You don't say it to [your boss]," or "If it's such a compliment, why don't you say it to [senior person the speaker respects]?"[11] Sometimes you will hear "What should I call you then?" You can say "[your name]," or "my name is [your name]." Sometimes you will hear the unbelievably silly "That's because he's not a bitch!" At that point, disengage.

If the speaker grumbles, "Fine, fine" or "Whatever" or some other concession or resentful non-apology, you may want to let the matter drop there. It's tempting to ask for an explicit apology: "Say you're sorry you called me a bitch." If you do, consider whether you are likely to get the apology, and how you will respond if the speaker says no. That said, this language shouldn't recur once you have asked for it to stop; see below under "What not to accept."

There is a line of thinking that the right thing to do about the term "bitch" is to reclaim it, to use it to describe oneself ("You bet I'm a bitch!"), and to greet other women colleagues with the term ("Hey, bitches!"). Used this way, the reasoning goes, the term loses its force as a weapon against women when women and, frequently, gay men use it among themselves. Whether you can effectively use it this way or not depends primarily on your workplace. Some workplaces will tolerate this kind of usage, and it may have the desired neutralizing effect on the speaker's use of that term. Many workplaces, however, won't tolerate it. Using the term in this way runs the same risk of engaging in an escalating match of personal remarks: the back-and-forth can escalate quickly to an uncomfortable level, and someone may get goaded into something

---

11. In his excellent book *The No Asshole Rule: Building a Civilized Workplace and Surviving One that Isn't* (New York: Warner Business Books, 2007), Robert Sutton lists two simple tests for determining whether a person is acting like an asshole. Here's test two: "Does the alleged asshole aim his or her venom at people who are *less powerful* rather than at those people who are more powerful?" (p. 9). I highly recommend this book for anyone trying to figure out how to interact with a difficult colleague.

unfortunate or unforgiveable. It has the further disadvantage that someone passing by may hear the exchange without context and conclude that neither party is behaving appropriately.

◆ **"Don't be so damn bossy."**

I sometimes call this term "junior bitch" or "bitch lite," as people often use it when they feel constrained not to say "bitch or "bitchy." (To be clear, it is good that they feel constrained not to say "bitch," if in fact that is the case.) "Bossy" is prominent in the US national dialogue about terms for women that insult them for the same traits praised in men.[12] When someone calls you bossy, you can ask "What do you mean?" Sometimes, both you and the speaker will be surprised by an answer: "Uh, I meant don't tell me what to do when I already know what my next task is." Now you have the benefit of an actual, addressable comment. You can say "You seemed not to know" or "My job is to review this week's tasks with everybody." Once you understand what the actual objection is, you can address that directly.

More often, however, "bossy" represents ruffled feathers: someone is not used to being told what to do at all, or by a woman; feels threatened by you and uses bossy as a put-down; feels threatened in general and takes it out on someone nearby, who happens to be you. The response "I am not bossy!" tends to lead to the childish "You are too!" kind of response. If you can, focus on the "Here's why I said [X]: do you disagree with what I said?" You will succeed to the extent that you can persuade your

---

12. See http://banbossy.com/, and the Twitter hashtag #banbossy. For a discussion of this issue beyond the term "bossy," see Nic Subtirelu, "Beyond *bossy*: More on our gendered characterizations of leadership and authority," *linguistic pulse: analyzing the circulation of discourse in society*, May 19, 2014, http://linguisticpulse.com/2014/05/19/beyond-bossy-more-on-our-gendered-characterizations-of-leadership-and-authority/.

colleagues to engage with the content of your remarks rather than their perception of your tone.

- After a contentious meeting, in which you have disagreed with a colleague, one of the meeting participants repeats to you that someone else said "She's just a bitch." Or "She's just bossy."

If remarks like these are repeated to you, the response "I'm sorry to hear that" generally works. You may or may not want to explore the motivation of the person who repeated the remark to you: "So, why are you telling me this?" If the messenger says "Oh, I just thought you should know what's being said about you," you can answer "Thanks, I guess" or "I'll take that up with [person who made the remark] directly, then." Whether you pursue this line of inquiry with the person who repeated the remark depends on what you think of his or her judgment generally: if he or she is reliable, you may want to ask.

As with responses to the remarks about body type, it is generally worth resisting the temptation to snap back "Yeah? He's a bastard" or "He's a prick, so we're even." A friend of mine who taught women's self-defense once told me "The thing that makes you feel best is not always the best or safest thing to do." It's natural to want to strike back when someone insults or overlooks you, or when you feel insulted or overlooked. Sometimes the snapback response takes the speaker aback, if he expected you not to reply, and sometimes it leads down a path of mutual insult that does not end well for anyone.

- "Don't worry about her bitching at you; she's a dyke."

"Dyke" and other equivalent terms for lesbians are frequently used as insults to describe any strong, competent woman, especially if she is single, whether she's straight or gay. How you respond to this depends on how fraught the term "dyke" is at your workplace. You should also consider whether there is an underlying question "Is she a lesbian?" and if there is, whether it is actually a question or merely intended as an insult.

If the remark is repeated to you, you can say "Really" or "I'm sorry to hear that," with the caveat that the latter response implies there's something unfortunate about being or being called a lesbian, even if you are responding to the part about "bitching" or to being spoken about behind your back. You can say "Why would anyone care?" if you are in a workplace where you reasonably expect no one would in fact care. You can also use the all-purpose deflector "Really?" or "Wow." You can use the humor of "I had no idea I'm a lesbian!" You can also say "True!"

If what you are experiencing is concerted anti-gay harassment, as opposed to a casual insult (though using this as a casual insult is bad enough) that is a much more serious matter, and you should consult your boss, unless your boss is the problem, and your HR representative, if you have one. See the section "What not to accept" at the end of this chapter.[13]

Physical presence and physical contact

This is a category of behavior that happens mainly with male colleagues. Most men are taller, stronger, and bigger than most women, and sometimes they exploit these physical differences, often without intending to or being aware they are doing so. Young women, particularly short young women, and to an even greater degree short young women with high-pitched voices, report these interactions frequently.

---

13. Anti-gay harassment at work is a serious matter. There are many resources to help you understand and decide how to address anti-gay workplace issues. One of the best is on the website of Lambda Legal: http://www.lambdalegal.org/issues/employment-and-rights-in-the-workplace.

- A colleague leans toward you in a meeting, raises his voice, and points at your face.

If the speaker is across the table, lean forward and look at the speaker's face; if he's next to you, sit up straight and look at the speaker's face. Don't raise your voice, and don't point back. Speak clearly, and stay focused on the subject at hand. You may want to resist the instinct to lean back away from the speaker, which may signal that you are intimidated, or you may want to lean back to send the message that the speaker is out of line.

- A colleague comes up close to you in your cubicle and looms over you, or looms over your cubicle wall.
- A colleague puts his feet up on your desk.

In the majority of cases, the looming behavior is unintentional. In those cases, you can stand up and suggest that you move to someplace where you can both sit down, or move to a meeting room or a space with a whiteboard. You can invite your colleague to sit down, if you have a second chair in your work area. You can use humor: "Ow, my neck! Have a seat, would you?" If someone sits too close, sit back. The classic you're-too-close gestures all help: crossing your legs, sitting up straight or slightly back, and crossing your hands on your knees or your arms across your chest. When the looming is intentional, all the same responses work. It may help in this case to move more quickly to business: "What can I do for you?" "What's up?"

When someone puts his feet up on your desk, you can ask "May I ask you to move your feet?" or told "Please move your feet" or "Move your feet" without the "please." You can put your own feet up on the desk, contact his feet, and say "Only room for one pair of feet here" and perhaps add "and those are mine" or "It is, after all, my desk."

♦ A colleague fiddles with your stapler, coffee mug, paper clips, or anything on your desk as he talks to you.

How you respond depends on whether this is nervous-tic behavior or intrusion into personal space. For the nervous crowd, for years I have kept a Slinky on the corner of my desk near the visitor's chair for people to fiddle with as they talk to me. Sometimes, in fact, this kind of small distraction allows the colleague to say what's actually on his mind.

Sometimes it's more personal, when, say, a colleague picks up a photo on your desk and says "So, a boyfriend?" You can answer straightforwardly, if you want to. You can use the "Let's stay focused, shall we?" approach, especially if you answered the direct question first: "What's up?" or "What can I do for you?" If you don't answer the direct question and your colleague insists on following up ("I asked if he's your boyfriend!") you can say yes or no, if you want; you can say "I'll tell him you asked"; you can say "Why do you ask?" Use the latter only if you want an answer or are prepared for and have the time for a few more exchanges.

♦ A new-to-you colleague or a vendor shakes your hand with unnecessary or painful force.
♦ The person shaking your hand in this way sees you wince or feels you react and smirks.

If this is done by a vendor, minus the smirk, or by an interview candidate, it is almost certainly a case of nerves. You may choose not to mention it at all. If the candidate says "So sorry! Don't know my own strength" or something like that and appears to mean it, you can answer "Oh, no problem."

If you get such a handshake from a colleague accompanied by a smirk, you can say "Ow!" or "You must lift weights" if you want to call attention to the unnecessary force. If instead you want to point out the assertion of dominance, you can say "Hey, we're not in the weight room" or "I'm not going anywhere; you can let go."

- A colleague declines to shake your hand.

If this happens, you may want to ask another colleague why; it's possible that the employee follows religious prohibitions about touching strangers or women in general or has a health condition that makes handshakes painful. If you find out there is no such reason, you may want to mention, in private, "I noticed you didn't shake my hand." You can leave it at that, with a question in your voice, and your colleague may tell you why. If you're aware that there is not a religious prohibition, you can use humor: "I do wash my hands routinely, you know." Be careful about using a humorous response if you aren't completely certain about any religious prohibitions or physical conditions.

- A colleague greets you with a hug, and lingers a little too long.
- A colleague pats you on the back, and his or her hand stays on your back a little too long.

How you react depends on how you interpret the action. From a much older or an excessively enthusiastic but otherwise benign colleague, you can simply smile and say "Hi!" If you want to put a little more distance in the remark, put a little more physical space between you by talking a half-step back more than you would ordinarily.

If you perceive the behavior as potentially intrusive—getting into your personal space in an unwelcome way, either as an assertion of power over you or as an unwanted pickup attempt—you can step back the extra half or full step before you respond and make your tone a little flatter: "Hello." If the person doing this has arrived for a meeting with you, sit across the table rather than next to him or her, especially in a meeting with more than the two of you. If this behavior occurs at an office social function and you want to avoid it, try circulating with others in a pair or small group, if possible; it's rare for the behavior to continue in front of a group, when the person exhibiting it is sober.

If you are at a workplace or social disadvantage—say you run a non-profit organization and one of your major donors indulges in these hugs at charity events for your organization—make sure you stay professional and, as soon as feasible, surround yourself with additional colleagues or other attendees.

- **Your norms about physical contact are different from your workplace's norms.**

You prefer less contact. Maybe you are not comfortable being touched by strangers at all, perhaps except for a handshake, or you have religious views that prohibit such contact, or a physical condition that makes it painful. You need two things: a standard greeting that you are comfortable with; most often in United Stated workplaces that is a handshake. You also need a standard explanation that you are comfortable with, especially if you prefer or need not to shake hands: "Wonderful to meet you; my neuralgia makes handshakes tough."

You prefer more contact. Let's say you are a hugger, or you have a particularly enthusiastic handshake where your left hand grasps the other person's elbow. For colleagues who are comfortable with that, you don't need to change your behavior. Some colleagues may interpret the behavior as unprofessional, however, and if you become aware of that reaction, ask someone at work you trust about how you are perceived. If you are new in your workplace, default to a straightforward handshake until you have enough experience there to know what the norms are.

Your job

This section is about workplace boundaries regarding what is and is not your job, and who gets to say what those boundaries are.

Your job is whatever I need you to do for me

This category of interactions occurs when a peer treats you as though you were responsible for tasks that are not part of your job. Most commonly, these are administrative, secretarial, or social tasks. This is a common behavior for much older male colleagues to exhibit around much younger women, though other colleagues of both genders do this as well.

- ◆ "Take notes, will you?" when it is not your standard job.

It's a good idea to have a dedicated note-taker at meetings, particularly meetings with a history of contention or a lack of follow-up. But it should not always be you if it isn't a routine part of your job. The first time you are asked, you may want to say yes, though with a phrase that proposed boundaries: "We should make this a rotating task, so there's always someone to do it." If you are consistently asked, suggest (again, if you haven't already) rotating the job. If your company supports collaborative applications like Google docs, you can propose creating meeting notes there so they are easy for everyone to edit and rotate note-taking duties, or so that every attendee can record her or his own contributions. If the requests persist after you suggest rotation, address it with the speaker privately after the meeting, making him or her aware of why you are asking to rotate the chore: "I want to be able to focus on the content of the meeting. I also want to make sure these kinds of jobs get rotated, so it isn't always or only me doing this."

- "Can you go get the client in the lobby and bring them to the meeting?"
- "Hey, will you order the wine for the company happy hour?"

These are tricky requests, as sometimes there is a time-sensitive aspect to them. If the client is in the lobby and the speaker is struggling to bring up the presentation on the laptop, you'll help out and go get the client. When these requests are repeated, only to you and other women colleagues, not to your male colleagues, you should address them with the speaker. In that case, you will need to answer like this: "no, sorry; I am also busy, with [X]." "No, I can't now, I am preparing for my [X] meeting." "Have you asked [colleague whose job it is]?" Remember, you are also busy with your job. Again, if you point to someone else to do the task, make sure it is properly that person's job. You may say this without "I'm sorry." If you have had this discussion with the same or other colleagues before, you probably should omit "I'm sorry."

There will be cases when the person requesting these kinds of things simply continues to do so, particularly if you have helped out before. From the speaker's perspective, why change what has worked? Then you may sit down with the speaker and say "I notice you have asked me to help you out with [task]. I am really busy with [most current task from your actual job]. Do you know that [colleague] can help you with that?" You may hear a response like "Yeah, but she wasn't around and you were." If you hear that or something like it, you will have to continue the conversation along these lines: "I appreciate the opportunity to help you, but I want to protect my own time to do [name a couple tasks or projects]."

If that does not work, or if you get a dismissive response, discuss it with your boss at your next scheduled time with him or her; if you don't have routinely scheduled time, set up a specific time to discuss it. Describe what happened and make it clear that you addressed the issue directly with the speaker but now need your boss's advice about how to proceed. Make it clear that you are trying to protect your time to do work your boss has already prioritized, and name specifically the tasks she or he values most. Don't go to the speaker's boss without consulting your own first.

Sometimes this situation is complicated when you actually like organizing workplace social events, such as group lunches or happy hours or the soccer team. As with taking notes, it is a good idea and a good skill to have, but it should not always be you who does it. Tasks like this should not fall into your lap by default simply because you are good at them and like doing them, if they are not otherwise part of your job. Much as you may dislike it, it may be worth letting a non-critical task go undone in some cases, to point out that the task needs to be explicitly assigned. Then you can engage in a discussion about whose job it is.

It's nobody's job, and therefore it's yours

As people take on jobs new to them, and especially as newer companies grow, they discover what is not getting done: someone needs to re-order office supplies, negotiate the lease renewal with the landlord, review the business license, pick up coffee for the break room, and on and on. If these tasks don't belong to someone already, they will often be dropped onto the nearest handy person, who is often the youngest woman in the office.

If this happens to you, the responses under "your job is what I need you to do for me" will work, with this addition: once you realize that a task is going to recur, talk to your boss about whose job it should be to do it, rather than *who* should do it. Talking about it as a job is the first step toward discussing whose job it should be, rather than it being someone's by default.

If a colleague asks you to take the task on, make it clear that you need to check with your boss first. If your boss asks you to add it to your responsibilities, you can either agree to take it on, or you can ask "How do you want me to prioritize [new task]?" If you add tasks to a work day and don't add any time to the day, then by definition something will not get done, or get done later than it otherwise would have. Make sure your boss understands what that looks like.

If the task is obviously well out of your job description, and no one else is being asked to stretch in this way, you can say "Can we make sure we rotate these kinds of jobs?" Or you can remind your boss that you took on the last such tasks, if you did, and ask if a colleague can take on that other one. If you adopt this approach, be ready for comments from your colleague about why you did it. To the colleague you can say "I took on [previous task], and I am getting behind on [actual job task]. We can rotate these things, you know, like [other shared tasks, if any]."

If you are the most junior person in the office, and picking up the coffee on the way into work is traditionally that person's job, then do it. Just make sure when you are no longer the most junior person that you hand over that task.

If you were hired because there were a lot of tasks not getting done, you are at particular risk for becoming a jack-of-all-trades (you also have the opportunity to develop a broad range of skills and contacts). That is fine if you were hired to be a jack-of-all-trades; you just have to make sure that your boss knows when you are getting overloaded and approves of how you are prioritizing. When you end up with a group of tasks that make sense to be consolidated into an individual person's single job, speak to your boss about redefining your job or hiring someone to do them. This process is the standard way that young companies realize they need someone to be their Facilities lead or manager. For employees who have absorbed these kinds of catch-all jobs, it's particularly important to keep a work diary (see under ***Ten workplace commandments*** below), as most people forget several items off long lists of smaller tasks.

You and I

These interactions expose the different assumptions of speaker and listener about what a particular comment or question means.

What you heard is not what I meant

This category of remark attempts to redirect the possibly uncomfortable discussion of what the speaker said to the less uncomfortable (for the speaker) discussion of what the speaker meant.

- "I didn't mean to offend you."
- "I didn't mean anything; 'girl' just means any woman."

The most important thing to realize here, long before you respond, is that you are not responsible for what a colleague intends. Moreover, someone's intention is unknowable, which is one reason many people appeal to their own better intentions when they realize a remark they made or something they did isn't appropriate. You are not responsible for knowing that someone's intentions are better than what that person says or does. You are, in fact, not responsible for knowing a colleague's intentions at all.

None of this means you might not choose to give a colleague the benefit of the doubt, because sometimes people make mistakes, and often they actually do mean well. You can ask directly about their intentions: "You implied that I'm not as competent as someone who went to [currently prominent program or school]. Did you mean that?" It also often works to repeat the language the speaker used: "You say you didn't mean that, but let me repeat what you said/did: [repeat it]." "I can't read your mind" often works and sometimes succeeds in reminding your colleague that you shouldn't have to try. Your colleague may be able to hear you if you spell out your inability to read her or his mind by saying "I am not responsible for your intentions; you said [what was said], and it was [how it was inappropriate]."

Notice the difference between these two formulations: "Did you mean to imply that I'm not as competent as someone who went to [currently prominent program or school]?" versus "I assume you didn't mean to imply that I'm not as competent as someone who went to [currently prominent program or school]. Am I right?" In the first case, the burden is entirely on the speaker to explain. In the second case, you have put yourself on the spot to interpret what the speaker meant. Both can be effective; the latter lets the speaker off the hook a trifle. Use either one as needed and effective, but be aware that they are different. In my experience, women, particularly younger women, often use formulations that make them more responsible in these interactions than they are, and let the person they are speaking to off the hook more than they should.

◆ "Oh, come on, I didn't mean that, I'm a nice guy!"

Sometimes it is helpful to focus on the speaker's expressed worry that you don't like him or her: "It's not that I don't think you're a nice guy; it's that I don't want you to ask me to do something you don't ask the guys to do." For the record, it matters much less to me if someone is nice than if someone is collegial. I don't need people I work with to be friends with me, though of course it can be fun and rewarding when they are, but I absolutely need them to be professional and collegial.

The exception to this approach is when the setting is a small business or workplace with a limited number of employees and low turnover. If you are in a workplace like that, especially with just a few long-tenured employees, it will probably matter much more that the speaker believes you do like him or her. Workplace dynamics are more critical and hard to avoid when there are very few employees than when you interact with many colleagues on a daily basis.

What you heard is not what I said

This category of response denies that what you said or saw was actually said or took place. In some cases it is honest disagreement about facts, which you can resolve. Sometimes it is denying something that clearly did happen with a snide remark, implying that you are not reliable in what you observe. At worst, it's insidious, undermining confidence and goodwill between colleagues.

- "Of course I didn't say that. I would never say anything like that."

This is a common thing to hear, generally right after you have called attention to whatever was said or done. Here's where repetition helps: "You said [X] to [Y] in [situation]." When someone greets you with denial, it's critical that you repeat the facts in their simplest form, in a neutral tone. Note the difference between saying "You said [X] to [Y] in [situation] versus "I heard you say [X] to [Y] in [situation]." The former focuses on the fact of what happened, whereas the latter focuses on your hearing skills. If you repeat the facts correctly, often the speaker will quickly shift to "That's not what I meant," in which case you can use the responses in the previous section.

- "You heard wrong."
- "That is not what happened. I can't believe you think that."

The difference between these two comments and the previous one is that these two put the burden on you: you made the mistake, not me. These remarks are, intentionally or not, more aggressive than the previous one. Again, repetition of what actually happened is critical here. It's important in this case to use focus on what the speaker did or heard: "You said/did [X]" rather than "Here's what I heard you say: '[X]'."

It may help to turn to or mention someone else who was there at the same time: "[Colleague] heard it too." This appeal can identify an ally, or a witness, but it has downsides: it puts someone else into the discussion who may not respond as you would like ("Personally, I'd drop it" would not help your cause with the speaker). And while it puts someone else on your side, it implies that you can't make your case alone. It may also make the speaker defensive to be called out in front of someone else, particularly someone who is respected.

- "What's the matter with women that they immediately leap to sexism? Geez, relax, would you?"

If the topic under discussion is a sexist remark or action, this kind of comment is often the next stage of a progression: first, "I didn't say that"; next, "That's not what I meant"; finally, "That's just what women always think." All these remarks represent ways to avoid personal responsibility for the remark or action in question. You should immediately focus, again, on what was actually said: "Here's what you said: [X]" If the speaker is upset, resistant, or angry, you may want to add "What did you mean?" or "what did you really mean?" These last remarks let the speaker off the hook: at bottom, you're calling out what they said or did, not what they mean, which is not knowable and not your responsibility.

- "I never said he called you a bitch."

In this situation, someone repeats a remark to you and, when you address the issue with the original speaker, the person repeating it gets caught as having violated the original speaker's confidence, having made a mistake, or having misrepresented the situation entirely. The person who repeated the remark then either gets asked why he repeated the remark or accused of misrepresenting what was said.

You have two people to deal with here: the person who repeated the remark to you, and the person who made the original remark. It's important to deal with them separately. The same responses to denials work in both cases: to the person who repeated the remark, "Here's what you said to me: [X]." When you do raise the issue with the original speaker, by the way, you may find a startled colleague who says "No, I never said anything like that!" In other words, the person who repeated the remark to you is trying to undermine you by telling you things that were never, in fact, said. It doesn't happen often, but you should be aware that it does happen.

You don't know what to say

One of the most disconcerting feelings in the workplace is to have an encounter with a colleague that leaves you without anything to say in the moment. I don't mean "I don't know," which is a perfectly reasonable response, though you should follow it with "but I'll find out and get back to you by [date/time]" or "but I'll find out and let you know as soon as I can when I will have an answer." I mean the interactions that, for one reason or another, leave you dumbfounded and, later, frustrated because you did not have the right response, or indeed any response at all at the time. You need a few standard, neutral things to say while you allow yourself to get over your shock, and then you need to decide how to follow up afterwards.

- "Why don't you know the answer?" (Looking at you, when it was someone else's job to find out)
- "Why did that process fail?" (Looking at you, when it's not your process)

Remember that the person speaking may simply not know that you aren't the right person to ask. In these cases, you need a two-part response: "I don't know, but I'll find out" or some variant of it is generally the first part, which may also include "I'll let you know what I find out by [date/time]." The second part, which you can put together with a little more time, can go like this: "I checked, and the person who knows best is [colleague]." You can then add whatever part of the answer you did get. Resist the urge to say "That's not my job!" or "It's not my fault!" You will find that "I can't answer, but [colleague] can" or "I have no idea, but let me find out" actually helps get to the answer and raises your credibility in the process.

- "I've never seen a woman do a good job at [task or role]."
- "God, she's ugly" (Said of another woman colleague, to provoke you and insult her.)

A common cause of being dumbfounded at work is a remark like these: one that seems so inappropriate that you can't imagine someone would think it, let alone say it. Even before you formulate a response, remember that when you hear things like this, you have a right to be horrified.

Here again a two-part response works. You can lead with a

standard "Wow" or "Really" or "Oh." Your inflection will tell the speaker if you mean "That's so bad I am not even going to dignify it by engaging with it" or "What on earth did you just let come out of your mouth?" Sometimes that will be enough to let the speaker know you believe he or she crossed a boundary. More selectively, you can actually say "What on earth did you just let come out of your mouth?"

The second part of the response depends on how well you know the speaker and the difference in age and status between you. You might choose not to follow up at all. If you decide to follow up, check with a couple colleagues first to see if this is a representative comment from the speaker. If you know the speaker well, you might choose to approach him or her afterwards and say something like "That comment you made/joke you told at the meeting was out of line" or "Did you notice how uncomfortable that joke/remark made everybody/[colleague]?" Be judicious about using the word "seem" and other phrases that take away the force of your comment: "It seemed to me people were uncomfortable" isn't the same as "People were uncomfortable." This conversation should not be about your discomfort; it should be about how the speaker caused discomfort.

No

You will hear no at your workplace a lot: "No, we can't approve [that project you like]," "No, you can't have that promotion, or new role, or raise," "No, you can't join that team or that project," "No, the company won't be funding [X benefit you value]," or "No, we're not going to hire that candidate you admired."

Sometimes "no" makes perfect sense: there aren't resources, time, or money to do everything, and some choices have to be made. Many times, particularly early in your career, you will not be the strategic decision-maker, and all of the reasoning behind the "no" won't be apparent to you; "no" is harder to take when you don't understand the reasons for it. Sometimes, in fact, the reasoning shouldn't be known to you, depending on how confidential it is.

There will be times when you believe you need to investigate and understand "no" when it doesn't make sense. Assuming you ask a person who has the right information, whether you get a satisfactory answer will depend on two things: whether you are perceived to have good motives in asking and whether you have a reasonable justification for asking.

- "Can you tell me why we decided not to approve [X project]?"
- "Can you tell me why we decided not to fund [this benefit]?
- "Can you tell me why we didn't hire [candidate]?"
- "Can you tell me why I didn't get to join that project?"
- "Can you tell me why I didn't get the same raise as [peer] got?"

All these questions depend on the assumption of your good intention for your workplace and for you; if you also start by believing you heard "no" because the alternative was better for the company, and what you want to understand is why, you are highly likely to get a good answer, one that satisfies you, or one that allows you to ask intelligent follow-up questions.

Before you ask your boss or anyone else about why you got a raise that differs from someone else's, be sure you know your workplace's protocol about such information. Some places are remarkably open about it, and others expect you never to mention anyone's salary unless they report to you, on the assumption that you would have no access to that information. If you are in such a workplace and you decide to raise this issue, you should begin by saying "I spoke to [colleague], who mentioned he got a raise of X% with a Y rating. I got a Y rating, but a raise of [less than X%]. Can you tell me why?"[14]

It is harder when the explanation for the "no" does not appear to make sense. Here, the most important thing is to ask the right follow-up question. As with your response to being invisible or ignored when you have something to contribute, the key is to have fact-based follow-up:

- "I was surprised when we didn't approve X project, when we approved Y that was projected to bring in less revenue."
- "We fund [this other benefit], which costs [$X] more, so I thought there'd be budget for [benefit I value] this year."
- "I was surprised when we didn't hire [candidate] when [other candidates] didn't seem any stronger, and [candidate I respected] had [this other skill]."
- "I thought I'd get a crack at this project because [peers] got the last [number] chances."
- "My understanding was that X rating meant Y raise, but my raise was [less than peer's]."

---

14. For a recent discussion of why secrecy about salaries works against women closing the pay gap, see Annie-Rose Strasser, "Why Obama is Ending Pay Secrecy for Federal Contractors," *ThinkProgress*, April 6, 2014, http://thinkprogress.org/economy/2014/04/06/3423399/obama-secrecy-salary/%E2%80%8B/. The 2011 survey on pay secrecy can be downloaded: Ariane Hegewisch, Claudia Williams, Robert Drago, "Pay Secrecy and Wage Discrimination," *Institute for Women's Policy Research*, June 2011: http://www.iwpr.org/publications/pubs/pay-secrecy-and-wage-discrimination When I arrived as a young faculty member at the University of Michigan, I was mortified to discover that, as a public employee, my salary was public information. Shortly after that, however, when I served on my department's salary review committee one year, I came to realize how valuable that openness was: it forced us to confront inequities much more quickly than if the information had been secret, because the committee members, and indeed all faculty members, knew that everyone knew and could come to the same conclusions themselves.

At some point in the discussion, if you do not persuade the person who made the decision to change it, you will have to accept that "no" is the answer. Now, however, you can ask another critical question: "What can I do now to [get desired outcome] next time?" A good boss will be glad you asked and will have answers, or won't have answers but will commit to getting them for you. When you hear them, write them down, repeat them to make sure you understand, and then send a confirming e-mail to your boss. Then follow up.

A bad boss will not have answers or won't share them and will not follow up promptly, if at all. In that case, you will need to decide if you can improve your work situation there enough to stay, or if it is worth staying even if things don't improve. If you want to stay, talk to someone you trust, inside or outside your workplace, about what you can do to make your situation better. If it is not worth it, make sure your résumé is up to date, your LinkedIn profile is current, and you know what you want to do next, either at that employer or somewhere else.

E-mail and texts

E-mail can exacerbate the difficult interactions I outline above. It can address many people at once with minimal effort, and adding to the conversational thread is as simple as hitting Reply All. Because recipients are not physically present, it tolerates a level of reply whose in-person verbal equivalent would ordinarily not be tolerated for a moment. Office shouters are routinely asked to calm down and counseled to behave differently, but people who type heated responses such as this one most often are not: "WHAT ARE YOU THINKING??!!??"

All of the responses I have discussed so far should, in theory, work in e-mail, except that many people do not read e-mails carefully, in their entirety, or in some cases, at all. In order to break through and make your responses heard, you need to take the conversation away from e-mail. As a general rule, do not send the fourth e-mail in the following thread: "[Foolish idea]." "No, definitely not [foolish idea]." "I SAID [FOOLISH IDEA]!" Instead, pick up the phone or walk to your colleague's desk. If that isn't immediately possible—say your colleague is several time zones away—offer to call him or her as soon as time zones allow and take the discussion out of e-mail.

As with e-mails, text messages can also complicate resolving the interactions like the ones outlined above, though for different reasons. Texts are subject to misunderstanding because abbreviations of standard English prose are the norm and their meaning is not always immediately obvious. Texts are also complicated because of autocorrect, and because they, like Twitter, lend themselves to being sent on the spur of the moment, without the pause for second thoughts and editing that seeing an e-mail on the screen can encourage.

Sensitive discussions shouldn't take place via text messages, where misunderstandings and anger escalate quickly. As with e-mail, the way to resolve these quickly is to pick up the phone if at all possible, or schedule time for a call. Texts are great for resolving yes/no questions quickly—"Did you get the data I posted?"—but not for long discussions. In general, if two or three text exchanges on the same thread don't clear up the matter at hand, you're better off calling.

Talking to your boss

Everything I have discussed so far applies equally well when the person you are talking to is your boss as when it is any other colleague. That said, there are some differences about talking to your boss in the context of workplace interactions that are worth bearing in mind.

Your boss will not know as much about your daily interactions as you will. He or she has both a set of peers and a job that are different from yours, and as such will not necessarily be privy to the daily details of your job: that's why he or she hired you. It is therefore up to you to give your boss enough context to understand what you are working on and dealing with.

Your boss is more senior than you are. Employees speak differently to more senior people, and if your boss is surprised that someone has treated you badly in some way, it may not be because your boss is an idiot, or blissfully unaware. It may well be because people do not treat him or her that way, or treat you that way in front of him or her. It is therefore up to you to give your boss concrete examples in a disinterested way.

Your boss has hired you to solve one or more problems and looks to you to come up with solutions. When you talk to your boss, avoid general statements with no proposed solutions from you: "Can you please help me with this jerk?" Instead, try something like this: "I have been having [this experience], which I have been addressing in [this way]. I'd value your advice on [this aspect of the problem]," which is much more likely to get a helpful response.

Finally, your boss has a boss, and loathes being surprised and therefore potentially surprising her or his boss. Don't surprise your boss: make sure she or he is aware of what you are working on, and what is getting in your way. Highlight issues and your proposed solutions to him or her early on; never go to someone else's boss without consulting your own first.

When your boss is the source of a problematic interaction, it is even more important than it is with other colleagues that you be fact-based and use a neutral affect. Women are perceived as being more emotional in their interactions than men, and whether that is true of you or not, you need to make sure that your interactions with your boss are as focused on work as entirely as they can be.

Inside the workplace

These interactions have as their root cause a standard workplace situation: an interview, a social event, a vendor demonstration in your workplace. They of course get worked out with a specific individual colleague, but the context of the situation influences how you engage.

Office décor

In this situation, one of your colleagues displays an item in his workspace that you find offensive: a pinup calendar, an offensive bumper sticker, and so on. In most medium to large companies, this is a matter for company policy, and you should consult your HR department. Odds are you won't be the first or the only one to call it out. If you are, and if you hear "Huh, no one else has said anything," whether that is correct or not, discuss with your HR representative whether the request to remove or conceal an item will be identified as coming from you (it shouldn't be). If the request will unavoidably be traced back to you, you need to decide whether you are all right with that and with what it will do to your work situation.

A different problem arises in smaller workplaces without such policies. It's particularly difficult when the person displaying something offensive has been at the company a long time, is considerably senior to you, or is your boss. A lot depends on how visible the item is, whether you also work in the same space, and whether customers can also see the item.

The simplest scenario is with items visible to clients: "Wow, don't let [X customer] see that" or, more neutrally, "is [X customer] going to be okay with that?" The answer might be "Yes." Unless the customer has expressed an objection to you, you might have to let it go at that.

If you consistently work in the same space with the item—say you share a square of four cubicles and it is in your line of sight on a daily basis—you can mention it in private: "It's hard to look at that every day." Here again note the difference between that statement and "I don't like looking at that every day," which puts the onus on you, as opposed to on the person whose item it is. The standard, silly comeback is "Don't look, then." To that you have some choices in your response: "How would you like it if I put up a photo of [comparably bad thing the speaker would dislike]?" This invites the speaker to take your point of view, but it most often does not work: you'll hear "Go ahead!" You could then actually put up such an image, if you want to, which makes your point better than the "How would you like it?" comment but may expose you to other unwanted commentary. It also may not solve the problem. Resist the temptation to post an image of the offending object to social media and say "See what I have to put up with at work?" (See the chapter **Life Outside of Work** for a more detailed look at the relation between your workplace and your social media presence.)

If it's your boss who has the offending item on display and you don't have an HR department to help you out, you are in a hard position. You can let it go, or you can say something, understanding that you risk alienating your boss. You may be able to address the issue indirectly: while away from the boss's office, or wherever the item is, you can say (if it's true) "Man, [key customer] is really sensitive about [issue relating to item on display]." The strong likelihood, though, is that the item will remain on display. If you believe this is likely, take it into account when you are deciding whether to raise the issue.

Office social events

Office social events come in three flavors: mandatory, optional in name but mandatory in fact, and truly optional, and which events fall into which category vary widely from workplace to workplace. Mandatory social events generally include such things as the company holiday party. The optional in name but mandatory in fact category includes any event which you can in theory choose not to attend, but it is clear that you are expected to show up, especially if you are in the relevant group: a trip to a baseball game for interns and their sponsors. Truly optional are informal events, especially those without company sponsorship, like a softball team.

The mandatory and optional-in-name-but-mandatory-in-fact events are the easiest ones to manage. Because they are sponsored by your workplace, and often held at the workplace, office rules of conduct generally apply, and the situations I discuss earlier in this chapter will also arise. The difference is often alcohol: if you or a colleague has more alcohol than can be gracefully handled, it can be difficult to maintain the standard of office behavior that you and your company are comfortable with.

- Said under the influence: "Hey, you're prettier than I thought" (No, I am not making this up)
- "You and I could probably have more fun someplace else"

If the attention is welcome, then it's welcome. If it is unwelcome, most women develop skills at fending off unwanted attention before they enter the paid workforce, and you can use some of those skills here. In an office setting, you need to preserve your self-presentation as a competent, pleasant co-worker at the same time that you fend off the intoxicated colleague. You can say "Why, thanks," to the first and "No, thanks" to the second in a tone that will make clear how unimpressed you are. You can also just say the same in a neutral tone, and move away from the speaker. You can mention your significant other, if you have one, or make one up, though you should be prepared to be challenged about his or her existence if your colleague flirts with you later on, when sober.

If the person flirting with you is your boss, you should be careful to make only the most neutral of remarks in an office setting, partly because your boss is your boss, and partly because your workplace may have guidelines about superior-subordinate relationships. If you don't already know what these are, find out, whether your boss's attention is welcome or unwelcome. The information will be useful in either case.

The most successful way to disengage quickly when these kinds of remarks are made is to travel in pairs or groups at these social events. Someone is much more likely to address an individual in this way than they are to speak to two or more people like this.

At optional events, where people regularly meet for a beer after work, say, or play softball one night a week in the summer, office rules are less likely to apply, and people make remarks and do things they would not normally say or do something within the workplace.

- "I always thought she had good legs." (said of someone in shorts)
- "I always thought she had good tits." (said of someone in a team t-shirt)

All-purpose neutrality works here: "Really" or "You don't say." Depending on how informal the setting is, you can be more sarcastic, or have a drier sense of humor, than usual. Do not, however, be under any illusions: what you say at an event where your colleagues are present, sanctioned by the office or not, will get back to your workplace.

If you are tempted to gossip—to respond by saying "Yeah,

but check out [other colleague]!"—you might not be kept in the speaker's confidence after the event is over, and you will certainly have established a reputation for gossip. Smaller workplaces and closer colleagues, however, often tolerate this kind of banter; if you engage in it, be sure you know ahead of time if your workplace does.

- "You should get out more; you're actually fun."
- "For God's sake have another drink and loosen up."

Again, most women learn to handle these remarks before they enter the paycheck workforce. If the attention is unwelcome, the keys here are polite repetition and being mindful that the remarks you make are all but certain to be repeated in your workplace. In some circumstances, that is not a bad thing, but you should also remember that what you say will not necessarily be what you are reported to have said.

Vendor demonstrations

In this situation, a vendor comes in to your workplace to demonstrate a new product or service. There are two different scenarios here: the vendor says or does something inappropriate, or one of your colleagues says or does something inappropriate to you in front of the vendor.

- "Are there any secretaries here who can help me schedule a follow-up?" (said by vendor to me, when I was the only woman and, as a vice president, the most senior person present)
- "Do you need the basic documentation?" (offering it to you in addition to the advanced system diagrams offered to your colleague)

Give the vendor the right information: "Yes, the person who can help you do that is [colleague]" or "[colleague] called the meeting, so I am sure she knows who will follow up." The good news is that since they want your business, vendors want to make you happy, so they are likely to respond to these cues.

- "You can send all the material to me; she doesn't need it." (Said to the vendor by a colleague)
- "I'll be making the decision." (Said to the vendor in front of you, as the vendor addresses you or gives you information)

You should follow up on remarks like these with your colleagues privately, out of the vendor's earshot. There are two reasons for this: one is that you will get better results from private interaction with your colleague, since often the reason for making such remarks is insecurity about competence, or the project, or reputation. The other is that you don't want to conduct company business, particularly problematic business, in front of an outsider.

In the case of the former remark, you can ask your colleague to send the material on to you afterwards. If you want to engage in the reason for the remark, you can ask "So why did you tell him to send the material to you?" There may actually be a good reason—say your colleague signed the nondisclosure agreement, which specified a limited audience for the material—and you should give your colleague a chance to articulate it. If there is not a good reason, you may hear "Uh, no reason," or "It was easier" or "Get over it." If the response is aggressive, you can respond with "Just do send me the information." You can say this in such a way that it is clear the data are more valuable than your colleague's good behavior, or you can say it more neutrally, as a simple reminder. Put a note on your calendar to follow up with your colleague to make sure you do get the information in case there is any pettiness around "forgetting" to forward it.

In the case of the latter remark, you can make sure it is correct. If you are actually the one making the decision, you should let your colleague know about it privately and follow up with the vendor afterward, by phone or e-mail: "Sorry for the confusion—I'll actually be making the decision. Please do send a copy to me." If your colleague is making the decision, you can ask for the information—"I can give you information for a recommendation once you get me the specs to review"—or ask "Why did you say that to him?" or "Why did you say that in that way to him?" The former works if the vendor was trying to figure out who the principal contact should be and was not clear about it; the latter works if your colleague was rude, or insecure and rude.

Interviews

As with vendor demos, there are two different situations here. In one case, a job candidate says or does something inappropriate. In the other case, one of your colleagues says or does something inappropriate to you or about you in front of the candidate.

The first case is usually relatively simple to address. If the candidate says something inappropriate, reply with a neutral "Really" or "Gosh" or "Wow." Note down exactly what the candidate said and make sure it is recorded in your feedback on the candidate and brought up when you discuss him or her. At the hiring meeting, you have to make your case about the candidate's remark: was it a warning sign, or bad enough to be disqualifying? Be sure to repeat exactly what the candidate said or did, and to contextualize it: was it the only remark or action of its type, or was it part of a pattern?

Colleagues may dismiss your concerns: "I don't think he'll do that when he's here" or "Maybe he was just nervous." Those are both possibilities, though it might be worth reminding your colleagues that people typically try to be on their best behavior in an interview, and they may adopt looser standards when they grow comfortable at work. You can ask the hiring manager, if it is not you, whether she wants that behavior in her group, or, to be less confrontational, if she thinks that behavior/that person will fit in on her team. A colleague out to annoy you may say, loudly, "Yes!"

Either the candidate will be hired or not: if not, it's no longer your problem. If hired, the candidate will either be a good employee or not. If she or he is a good employee, it's no longer your problem or indeed anybody's problem at your workplace. If not, then you have the start of a record where you noted a problematic encounter.

There is at least one case in which a candidate saying something inappropriate might not be a straightforward situation, and that is when the candidate is friends with or related to someone senior at the company, or has been given an interview because of a relationship with someone senior at the company. If that is the case, be careful to record exactly what the candidate said, and limit your editorializing in your interview feedback. Nobody wants to be associated with hiring someone who will reflect badly on the workplace, and odds are that an off-putting candidate will not be hired.

The situation is different when it is your colleague, rather than the candidate, making an inappropriate remark. For instance, if you are interviewing as a team and your co-interviewer says about a comment you just made "We really don't handle those kinds of issues here much, anyway; what do you think about [this other thing]?" You should address this privately with your colleague after you are out of the interview: "When you said 'we don't see those kinds of issues here much,' I was thinking about [example of that issue]. What did you mean?" The key here is to focus first on the issue, not on your colleague contradicting you publicly. Once you find out what your colleague meant, you can raise the other issue: "Even if you don't think it is as common as I do, we should discuss that kind of thing out of the candidate's hearing."

Requests for donations

Requests for charitable contributions come frequently at workplaces, everything from requests that you buy Girl Scout cookies, support the company's charitable efforts, or help with a cause dear to a particular employee.

For small purchases, like cookies or raffle tickets, you can say "Yes," if you are so inclined. Your request for $5 of tickets or one box of cookies may be met with "Geez, how about a little more?" In this case, you can say "Okay" if you feel like it or "No, thanks." Beware of saying "Not today" or "Not this week" or "Not this pay cycle" or "Geez, I just can't right now" or any other remark that references a time frame, as the seller may view that as an invitation to follow up with you in the next cycle.

You can say "No, thanks," which you can follow with "I already bought cookies from [kids at grocery store, neighborhood kids, etc.] You may justifiably feel you should not be required to excuse or explain yourself, and if you don't want to, you don't have to. You may hear in response "[Last person to have your job] always bought a bunch." You can say "That's great; [repeat what you said]." or "I appreciate you thinking of me, but no thanks." Avoid saying "Not today" and so on for the reasons noted above.

How you respond to requests to participate in company charitable efforts depend on whether they take place during or after work hours. If they are during work hours, you probably need to participate to the same extent as your colleagues (but see below about charitable efforts to which you have a particular objection). If it is after work hours, you can say "I need to check my home calendar/with my spouse." Be prepared to have a different answer when the asker comes back, so it doesn't seem as though you are making up excuses. In the meantime, check with other employees about whether this activity is voluntary, voluntary in name only, or mandatory.

A more difficult situation comes up when someone asks you to support a charity near and dear to his or her heart that isn't company-sponsored. The same responses for saying yes or no to donations in the form of small purchases work, with two exceptions: when it's the boss's personal charity or favorite cause, or when the charity supports a cause to which you are opposed.

In the case of your boss's charity (as opposed to a company-sponsored one), you can say yes, if you are so inclined. If you are not, for whatever reason, tread carefully when you say no: "Gosh, I'm flattered you asked, but I have to say no thanks." Your boss ought to realize his or her power over an employee (and in my opinion ought not to have asked in the first place) but if she comes back with "Why not support [X]?" you can say "I already have a charity I focus on" or "We just can't" or "We just can't right now." If you hear in response "Hey, I know how much you make, remember?" you are being warned to contribute.

If the charity supports a cause to which you are opposed, you should decide whether you want to state the reason for your opposition. You may find yourself offending the person asking—presumably she supports the cause, or at least doesn't object to the part you oppose—so you may want to qualify your no in this case: "I'm really focused now on [other good cause] through [charity]." If you say why you are opposed, be careful not to blame the person for her choices: "I'm vegetarian, so a sustainable poultry farm isn't really my thing."

Sometimes the request is for a charity that supports a house of worship. If you decline to donate, it may be assumed you don't support some aspect of the sponsoring religion. That could be true or not. If you are specifically asked about your opinion ("So, do you have a problem with [religion]? Is that why you won't donate?"), you can answer honestly and explain what you do not support. You can also deflect the question: "No, I have [another charity]" or "I guess nobody is going to agree about everything." In either case, reply in such a way that you are not perceived to be passing judgment on a religion or its adherents wholesale. No matter how carefully you phrase your comment, however, you may be perceived as doing just that.

Saying no to requests for political contributions can also be hard, for many of the same reasons that declining to support a religious charity is hard. The most sensible thing is a no-solicitation policy at work or during work hours for any political cause, and if you are asked to make such a contribution, you should check on your company's solicitation policy. As with a charity supporting a cause you oppose, if you say no, be careful not to imply personal criticism of the person asking: "Oh, no thanks," "No thanks, not now," "No, that isn't really my thing."

Be careful of the remark "I'm not really engaged politically," as it tends to kick off a discussion about why you should be politically engaged, particularly with colleagues motivated enough to be collecting money for political causes.

When people leave

Departures from the workplace can be occasions for celebration and best wishes: an anticipated retirement, a departure to start advanced training, a relocation with a spouse. They can also be hard: a relocation with a spouse to an unknown place, a departure owing to a layoff, a termination for cause, or a voluntary departure from a bad work situation.

The celebrations and best wishes are relatively easy: you congratulate your colleague, and if she or he wishes, you exchange contact information. The departures that are involuntary or under pressure are harder. When it is your colleagues who are leaving, you should expect them to be stressed, maybe shorter-tempered than usual, and worried about the future. Cut them some slack if their interactions are rougher around the edges than you are used to. If it is a colleague you value, you can offer to stay connected on LinkedIn and to pass on any job leads or news you might hear of.

Typically the difficult interactions around departures fall into two categories: reassurance and vindictiveness. In cases where people are fired or laid off, you may hear "Geez, did I do that bad a job?"

In this case, you can say "Your skills and the company aren't a great match." Be careful about saying that the departing employee's skills and his or her boss's needs aren't a good match. A remark like that could be true, or not true, but it may get back to the employee's boss, who may be your boss one day. Always be aware that, however obvious the reasons for the employee's departure may be to you, they may not be obvious to the employee. It's also likely you are not privy to all the details about his or her job situation.

In the case of a layoff owing to a loss of business or a change of company direction, you can say "It's not you; it's where the business is right now" or "This is bad luck, is all." You should be wary of saying things like "everybody's going through it all over the place; this isn't just you." It sounds helpful in that it isn't the employee's fault, but it isn't helpful in that it makes it sound as though there are layoffs everywhere and it will be hard to get a job. And even if it isn't just that employee, and even if misery loves company, nobody else is responsible for paying that employee's bills.

Vindictiveness is harder to address, whether you sympathize with the departing employee or not. You may hear "If I'd been given a decent project, ever, I could have shown them what I can actually do."

Since such remarks concern the now-unchangeable past, it's tempting and easy to engage in the game of what could have been.

You may find that it helps the employee to vent for a while: "You are right; this sucks." "I am so sorry this happened. It just stinks." If the past or present is too distressing to discuss, you can start to make remarks about the future: "I am so sorry this happened. You are going to be totally great at your next gig." "You are going to get a great thing, and then you will show them."

- "[Boss] is a total bastard, and I'd still be there if I worked for a sane person."
- "[Company] is run by morons."

If you agree with these statements and believe it is not just about this one employee, you should be revising your résumé, practicing your interviewing skills, and looking for another job. What you should be saying to him or her, however, should be more positive and focus on the future: "Your next boss is going to be way better for you, I'm sure." It isn't your job, or at this point even kind, to point out everything the departing employee could have done better or everything the company could have done better or differently; support comes in the form of describing how much better this individual's situation can get.

If, on the other hand, the individual is really ready for a conversation about how to make his or her own situation better, you will be asked something like this, generally a few days or weeks after the departure itself: "I really don't want this to happen again. What do you think I should change next time around?" These questions are rare, and when they are asked, you can respond honestly.

- "Wait until they hear what I am going to say about them."

This kind of statement is perfectly understandable, but acting on it is a terrible idea. Most people end up changing jobs, and often careers and fields, quite a bit over the course of their working lifetimes.[15] When someone says something like this, you can respond "Well, just take care of yourself right now. Don't post anything about the company that you'll regret later, you know?" "This company/boss isn't worth that kind of risk" or "You're going to get another job, and then this will matter way less in the rearview mirror." Most people calm down and act sensibly out of self-interest, not wanting to become unlikable to their next boss.

When you are the departing employee, for whatever reason, the trick is to act as though your next boss were watching. You want your next boss to see you as his or her next good hire: someone who will do good work, someone who was so good a colleague at your previous jobs that talented people will want to go to your next workplace, and someone who burned no bridges so previous customers will continue to want to work with you. Here are some phrases that may help: "Thanks, I'll miss you!" or "Thanks, good luck!" works for anyone you'll miss. "Thanks, goodbye!" works for anyone you won't.

Small workplaces

Some of the advice I give in this chapter works better in larger workplaces than in smaller ones. In smaller ones, everyone may have the same boss, work in the same small space, and share many of the same tasks, even if they have different jobs. Those workplaces often lack the so-called support functions of larger companies: there is no designated administrative person, no IT function, and no HR. In these circumstances, how you get along

---

15. The Bureau of Labor statistics issued a report on the number of jobs held by the youngest baby boomers, born from 1957–1964, and the number, 11.3 jobs, shows that workers of this generation changed jobs much more frequently than you would think, even discounting early lower-wage jobs. "Number of Jobs Held, Labor Market Activity, and Earnings Growth Among the Youngest Baby Boomers: Results From a Longitudinal Survey," Bureau of Labor Statistics, July 25, 2012, http://www.bls.gov/news.release/pdf/nlsoy.pdf.

with your colleagues will be even more important to your and your company's success than in larger workplaces.

If you are in a small workplace, when issues like the ones I discuss here arise, you should address them sooner rather than later. In small workplaces, it is tempting to let disagreements slide in order to preserve camaraderie, or to not let the discussion take up time in the face of the looming deadline your small team faces. Counterintuitively, it is even more important in those situations to address issues promptly than it is in larger workplaces, because you all rely so heavily on each other. The power of one individual's assumptions looms large on a five-person team: "Someone else usually takes out the trash from the break room." Those assumptions loom even larger when they are unspoken.

In these cases, where almost everyone is doing at least some of the administrative and janitorial tasks, the easiest way to prevent resentment and bad feelings is to rotate all of these tasks and to put the rotation on a calendar that everyone can see, either an electronic shared calendar or a posted printed calendar. The easiest way to institute and maintain this is to sit down at specified intervals, say every Friday just before everyone leaves, and go over the calendar of tasks for the next week.

Another characteristic of small workplaces is their tendency to normalize certain behaviors. In a five-person office, if four people play music after work, they will ask job candidates whether they play an instrument. The power of exclusion is strong on small teams: the non-musician or non-rock-climber will both stand out more and potentially feel more self-conscious about it. It often helps to address this directly when hiring a new person, which in small workplaces tends to be a big deal. In response to "Are we sure [candidate] will fit in?" it's worth asking "Why wouldn't she?" and making sure that the reasons are more substantial than "I wish she wanted to go rock-climbing with us." You can frame the question in terms of compatibility, which is critical in workplaces, versus conformity, which isn't, and which, in fact, tends to narrow the pool of ideas, inspiration, imagination, and experiences available to your team.

Outside the workplace

Outside the workplace, you lose some of the context that you and your colleagues normally have with each other. At trade shows or local business lunches, other people see you and your colleagues but don't know how you usually behave with each other; they do, however, have their own ideas about how you should behave. So what you say to a colleague at those times will differ from what you say in the workplace, in that you will typically save some comments for later, when you are not surrounded by people who may not know how you ordinarily interact.

In addition, work-related travel brings with it all of the interactions of the workplace, plus the stresses of travel, an extra dose of fatigue, and the potential for employees to view their after-hours time as free from normal workplace constraints. Before you go, find out what the expectations of the trip are: who you will be meeting, what your company wants out of the meeting, what your boss wants out of the meeting, and what the standard company code of conduct is on the road. For example, some or all of the following may apply: no alcohol at lunch but at dinner it's all right, employees must/must not share hotel rooms on the road, entertainment expenses are/are not reimbursable (and you'll need to clarify what falls under "entertainment").

Trade shows and other business events

At trade shows, you, your colleagues, and your company are in front of dozens, hundreds, or thousands of potential customers. It's critical to represent your company well.

- Your colleague at the booth tells an off-color joke, to roars of laughter from the people listening
- "I can give you better information about our product line," said to a customer in front of you

Speak to your colleague afterwards, out of earshot of anyone at the show. You can say something like "I don't know if you noticed, but [one of the people in the audience] seemed really uncomfortable with that joke you told" or "What was up with that joke? I don't think it went over well," especially if the audience was more than a few people. If your colleague says "Oh, I don't think so" or "I'm sure it was fine," you can say "Hope you're right, but why chance it?" You will be more successful pointing out your audience's reaction than referring to any company rules your company has, which can make your colleague worry that you might snitch on him. If your colleague is senior in your organization, or it was your boss who told the off-color joke, you may want to wait to get back to consult someone else at work.

In the second case, you can use the same remarks that apply to an interview in which a colleague says something inappropriate: tell your colleague that you want to make a good impression on customers and potential customers. If he made the remark in front of a woman, say that you want customers to think that he is someone they could work with.

Depending on what was said and how the potential or current customers reacted, and whether the remarks are characteristic of this particular colleague, you may want to discuss the interactions when you get back to your workplace with your boss or some neutral party at work whom you trust.

- You and some of your colleagues are attending a local business association luncheon in your town, an industry luncheon in your field, or a fundraising breakfast for a cause your company supports. The master of ceremonies stands up and proceeds to tell jokes: one in which a woman is shot, one in which a woman is beaten until comatose by her husband, and one in which an old, sex-starved woman is confused with a rabid dog. (No, I am not making this up, either.)

If the speaker works at your company, you can discuss the incident with your HR department, if you have one, or with your boss, if you don't. If the speaker is your boss, you need to consider whether he is likely to appreciate feedback (by which I mean understand his behavior is inappropriate and change it), or appreciate it from you. You also most likely need to be updating your résumé.

If the speaker does not work at your company and you are alone at the event, you can tell whoever is in charge of sending people to the event, and, if your company is a named sponsor, ask whether your firm wants to be associated with someone who talks like that. Be prepared to hear "Oh, he always tells those jokes, has for years." You can say "Wow, I wonder how they went over with all the other women there" or just "Wow" or "Really" or "Too bad."

If you're not alone at the event and one of your colleagues laughs at a joke you find offensive, you can take up the matter with him or her afterwards: "Wow, that joke was awful." If he says, "Yeah, I just laughed because everyone else did," you can agree, disagree but let it go, raise your eyebrows, or use an all-purpose response: "Huh."

- A colleague says to you "Oh, he must have thought you were my girlfriend."
- A colleague repeats a remark to you: "[Other person] said he thought you were my second wife."

You can use an all-purpose neutral response, with tone calibrated to how relatively odd you perceive this remark to be: "Really?"

or, more repressively, "Really." If you say "I can't imagine why [other person] would say that," be prepared for an answer that you may not like, and possibly for an extension of the conversation. If you believe this is the opening gambit of an unwelcome pickup attempt, you can say "Be sure to tell him no." You can say "I have a significant other/spouse" or "I hope you told him I have a significant other/spouse." These last responses have the disadvantage of perhaps seeming to your colleague to invite inquiry about the relative seriousness of your personal relationship, even if you don't intend that.

Other than the "Are you available?" subtext of these remarks, they may also be intended to categorize you as not really part of the workplace: you are arm candy coming along to the conference or trade show, but certainly not a sales support engineer in your own right, for example. If you believe that is your colleague's intent, steer the conversation back to work.

Recruiting events

As with interviews, the critical thing here is presenting your company professionally to potential job candidates. In industries where there is competition for talent, these job fairs are vital to your company's success. Your HR or recruiting team, if you have one, will often have a code of conduct for these events. For example, when I attended these on behalf of a large company, we were told the following: "No off-color jokes; no foul language; no remarks of any kind about a candidate's race, ethnicity, religion, gender, or sexual orientation; no remarks about competitors; no asking a candidate out."

♦ [Your colleague at the booth tells an off-color joke]

Your reaction depends on the age difference between your colleague and the candidates. If your colleague is much older, you may want to say something like "That joke didn't seem to go over with one of the candidates." If he dismisses you as not understanding how guys talk to each other, you can say "Maybe, but not everybody thinks exactly the same about that kind of thing."

◆ [Your colleague at the booth pays much more attention to male candidates, and brushes off the women]

If you and your colleague are equally responsible for reviewing the résumés and speaking to the candidates, you can decide to pay attention to the women if you colleague isn't. If he is principally responsible for deciding whom to invite for an interview, you can say "Make sure you check out [names of candidates]: I talked to them and they're really good." If he dismisses them, call attention to the strongest features of their résumés. If you have someone from recruiting with you, make sure she or he sees the names of the candidates you think are strong.

When you get back to your workplace, you can check whether the names of the strongest candidates got to the right hiring managers. You can say things like "I saw a bunch of great people, especially [names]." If the hiring managers say "Who? I never saw their résumés," be sure you can say "Yeah, I thought they fit our profile for A, B, and C reasons." The need for talent should prompt the hiring manager to follow up with whoever is in charge of getting them the résumés from the event and confirm that they are good candidates.

Client demonstrations

Demonstrating your company's product or service, or showing a project in development to a customer, is one of the most critical interactions your company will have with customers or potential customers. As a result, there's usually a lot of pressure to do well. People react to pressure in different ways, and not always as you would like. The single most important thing you can do to ensure success (aside, of course, from you and your colleagues' doing good work) is to rehearse: have someone play the client in a role-playing exercise and identify and agree in advance exactly what role you and your colleagues are to play when you are in front of the client.[16]

- "I'll be the one in charge of [phase]," said to the client, when you have agreed on some other role for him.
- "She'll be doing [role]," said to the client, when you have agreed on some other role for you.

In both of these cases, make sure the client gets the facts. If it appears to be just a slip, and you can get the correct information out quickly, do that: "Oh, actually, it'll be [other colleague] doing that." Probably your colleague will agree, if it was just a mistake. If he was trying to take credit, or if the flow of the conversation is such that you don't want to interrupt the discussion with the customer, wait until afterwards and then say, out of the customer's earshot, "We agreed ahead of time that you would do [role] and I would do [other role]; is there a reason to change?" Note the difference between saying simply "We agreed" versus "I thought we said . . ." or "I remembered we agreed . . ." Talking about your memory allows your colleague to say "You misunderstood" or "I didn't say that" or "you're not remembering right."

As you rehearse your presentation, make sure you have someone play the role of the customer and ask a range of questions. You

---

16. Agreement starts at a meeting where everyone who will be going to the client is present. If you don't already know each other, introduce yourselves, and say, out loud (not assume) what each person will be responsible for at the meeting, including taking notes, answering key questions, and sending follow-up responses after the meeting. See the excellent discussion of how and why this exercise is critical to team success in Atul Gawande, *The Checklist Manifesto* (New York: Henry Holt, 2009), 103–11.

should also agree on who is best suited to take which questions, so you don't interrupt your colleagues in front of the customer.

WHEN IT DOESN'T WORK

Sometimes, no matter how skilled you are at your job, how good your interpersonal skills are, or how much you practice the responses I discuss, the advice I have given you won't work. After trying many different things on different occasions, the difficult interactions or objectionable behavior continues. Now what?

I return to the analogy of business-continuity planning that I made at the opening of this chapter, where you have a range of approaches available to you: prevent, mitigate, prepare, and accept. Just as almost all business-continuity planning involves a combination of these approaches, dealing with persistently troublesome workplace interactions does as well.

For the sake of this discussion, I assume prevention has not worked: you have tried these interactions and they have failed. That said, from time to time you should keep doing them, if for no other reason than to point out, to you and to your colleague, that you still notice the problem.

Mitigation in this case means lessening the effect these interactions have on you. For your own mental health, as you get more used to them, presumably you will be less surprised by them, which takes away part of the difficulty. You should remind yourself that you cannot change people, and that only they can change their behavior: don't let yourself slip into pursuing the fruitless goal of changing someone else. For your workplace health, you should take up particular difficulties with your boss, so she or he knows you are having this trouble and can advise you. It's also important to document, in conversation, in e-mail, and writing if need be, that this trouble exists, so that there is a record at performance-review time.

Preparation means practicing, applying, and refining the kinds of responses I discuss here, as well as working on the longer-term skills I discuss in the next chapter, **Planning Ahead**. It also means engaging with your colleagues to help you. Describe your interactions to a trusted colleague or mentor, and get their advice. If you have a critical presentation coming up where a difficult colleague will be present, practice with someone who knows that colleague (or, better still, can convincingly role-play him or her). Talk to other colleagues who have had trouble with that individual—you are almost never the only one—and discuss what has worked for them. Support each other: you can say of colleagues who are overlooked "Let's ask [colleague]; she had a really good idea when [similar problem] came up" and "Try [colleague], who is great with this customer."

The final approach, acceptance, is in many ways the least satisfying to you personally and the least useful to your workplace, because the problem is not solved. Suppose you have done what you can, including preventing it from derailing your work and preparing for the next iteration. The next step is to accept that a particular interaction with a particular colleague will not improve, so that you can focus your time and effort where you can make a difference.

That said, some situations you cannot accept, either when they persist or the first time they occur; that is the topic of the next section.

WHAT NOT TO ACCEPT

Most of the situations I have discussed so far, and many others like them that you will run into over the course of your working life, are products of ignorance, thoughtlessness or a bad day at work or home, rather than someone who actively and personally dislikes you, all women, all women in the workplace, or all women in that particular workplace. And while not everyone enjoys, or even tolerates, having their behavior challenged and changed, most people are, in the end, reasonable, and want a workplace that works for them and the company and all the employees in it. You should always assume good intentions, and most of the time you will be correct.

There are, however, some things that aren't well-intended, and some that, whether they are well-intended or not, aren't generally acceptable in the workplace. Many workplaces, particularly larger corporate workplaces, define what is and what is not acceptable in a code of conduct. It is typically maintained by HR, Legal, or both, and almost always discussed during new-hire orientation. If you work at such a company and don't know whether you have one, or don't remember what is in it, ask your HR representative. If you work at a company without a code of conduct, you will have to rely on whatever guidance HR or your boss can give you.

The first thing you have to consider with these most problematic interaction is whether to engage at all, and if so how much. You have a couple of key decisions to make: will this person retaliate against you, and if so, what will the consequences be? Can you afford to address the situation at all? If, for example, you live where it may be hard to change jobs, or find any other job; if you are the primary or sole breadwinner, and you cannot afford to be out of work; if your wages are such that losing even a day's pay is a hardship, the risk of addressing someone's bad behavior may be too great for you to go forward.[17] If you decide you cannot go forward, for any of these kinds of reasons, remember that your

---

17. If you are in such a situation, the best written guidance I know for day-to-day survival tactics is the chapter "Tips for Surviving Nasty People and Workplaces," in *The No Asshole Rule*, 127–54.

inability to get away from it does not make the behavior any more acceptable.

If you decide you can go forward, here is some guidance. Workplace behavior you should not accept ranges from the inappropriate to the dangerous. Inappropriate behavior is most often some combination of persistent, personal, and unwanted: a colleague keeps asking you out, after you have made it clear you are not interested; a colleague makes degrading personal remarks about your body type, dress, or sexual attractiveness, often under guise of "compliments" after you have requested that the remarks stop; a colleague persistently tries to engage you on social media after you have declined; a colleague uses derogatory terms for your religion or sexual orientation or race. In an earlier section I discussed "That's not what I said," which is most often a disagreement or a dodgy rhetorical device to evade responsibility. When it's a concerted strategy, however, it is called gaslighting, and in its extreme form it is a classic tool of abusers and bullies.

When threats of consequences are added, inappropriate behavior turns much worse: "Sleep with me or I'll tell the boss your work stinks." "Stay late to help me with my work or I'll tell everyone you're a bad colleague." Implicit threats are also threats, by the way, as when a colleague uses a derogatory term to you or in your presence, and looks at you and smirks, implicitly daring you to do something about it. Finally, it turns dangerous when there is a physical threat, to you, your family, or your property.

Perhaps counterintuitively, the first thing you have to do once an incident is over is write down what happened, whether that is notes on paper or in a text file or a document on your mobile device. No doubt you wish you did not have to deal with it further, and you may justifiably resent having to deal with it at all, even by writing it down. But you should set down, in very brief notes, who said or did what to whom, when, and under what circumstances. If it happens again, add to your initial notes and date the new information each time. Do not rely on your memory alone: these interactions are stressful, and under stress, no one's memory is as reliable as it otherwise might be. And you will not want to think about the behavior any more than you have to; writing it down will lessen the anxiety that comes reminding yourself of the incident lest you forget details when you are asked.

Next you have to decide whether there is anything to be gained by speaking directly to your colleague. If you have already done that, and the behavior continues, it is unlikely that re-engaging will change matters. If you have not already done that—say you have heard someone refer to you as a fat lesbian or a skinny bitch—then you can start by asking your colleague to stop using the offensive term the next time you hear it. It's entirely understandable that you might not want to speak to your colleague about this at all, though if you do, you may hear "I had no idea she'd care" or "I had no idea anyone objected to [offensive term]."

Once you have spoken to your colleague, make sure the right people in your workplace know what happened. You should let your boss know, unless your boss is the person making the remarks, in which case you should speak to HR. If your boss is the source of the comments or the behavior and you don't have an HR department, you should speak to the most senior colleague whom you trust. When you discuss the matter with that person, whoever it is, make sure you have all the facts: who said or did what to whom, when, and under what circumstances. You will need those notes you took.

The goals here are twofold: one, to make the inappropriate, threatening, or dangerous behavior stop; two, to preserve your position in your workplace. By position, I don't just mean you have a job, but that you are thought of as a good colleague doing a good job. You will often find that you are not the first person to resent certain behavior from a particular colleague, though you may be the first person to ask your firm to take official notice of it.

WHEN TO LEAVE

As I was writing this book, one of my early readers noted that I occasionally advise women to update their résumés and look for another job in certain circumstances. His feedback was interesting: "I think women in these circumstances should stay and fight to make it better!" The question is, when is that true, and more importantly, when is that true for you?

At some point, an interaction like the ones I have described may become so problematic or so persistent that you find yourself considering whether you should leave your current workplace. There are many other reasons to leave—you're bored, you've grown out of the job, you're marrying and moving away, you're going back to school—but I am talking about only those departures influenced or decided by these inappropriate interactions. There isn't an answer that covers every circumstance, or even most, but here are some things to consider.

If you have tried for a while and you are not seeing the changes in behavior that you want to see, ask yourself how much you are willing to put up with to do this job. How much you like or want or need the job? How much you like the workplace? How important the job is to your career? Consider how much of your mental energy is being spent on these interactions, and decide if it is a tolerable amount. Consider how much of it is spilling over into life outside of work, and decide if you are all right with that amount.

If the behavior you find troubling, or persistent, comes from the leader of the company, or its most respected employees, or your boss, you should consider how likely it is to change, or how likely it is that the people exhibiting the behavior will leave the company. In smaller workplaces, in locations with fewer companies and opportunities, or in situations where the person causing the problem has a large personal or financial stake in the workplace, the answer may be "Not very." In that case, you should do what you can to make yourself ready for your next job (see "Make yourself ready for your next job" in *Ten workplace commandments*).

If the behavior is personally threatening, particularly if it is physically threatening, and if it is being minimized or ignored by your management, you should prepare yourself as promptly as you reasonably can. "As promptly as you reasonably can" may not be any time soon, but when you are not taking immediate action, you can still make preparations for getting new skills and making new contacts. In this particular circumstance, it's critical that you have a good basic understanding of your finances (see **Life Outside of Work** below).

Planning Ahead

MAYBE YOU HAVE read through all those scenarios in the last chapter, evaluated possible responses, dismissed some out of hand, considered others, and tried a few. If so, you may now be thinking "Yeah, but what can I do so this stuff doesn't happen in the first place?"

My answer has some unsatisfying aspects to it. Much of what drives the workplace interactions described in the previous chapter is beyond your or any single individual's control. Societal forces that socialize men and women differently, deep-seated, long-held biases against women in many fields, media portrayals of men and women that reinforce certain stereotypes about what people can and should do are all part of the greater economic and social landscape within your workplace, where you and your colleagues must function. You work within the environment that colleagues help create, and what they help create is not always as you would have it, to put it mildly.

Along with thinking "How can this stuff not happen in the first place?" you may also be asking "What will make [colleague] change?" The answer to this is also unsatisfying: you cannot change a colleague's behavior. Along with nearly every relationship expert on the planet, I encourage you to stop thinking in terms of how you can get your colleagues to change, and start thinking in terms of their changing how they treat you, and how you can influence them to do that.

All of this is not to counsel despair that the changes need to be bigger before anything gets better. I contend that changes in the way we deal with the kinds of daily interactions I describe here contribute to larger-scale changes. Women want to see workplaces in which we don't hear "bitch" or "bossy" applied to a woman, in which people don't assume women are the secretaries rather than the managers, and in which we are evaluated on the same basis as our male colleagues. I urge you to remember that your workplace interactions take place in a broader context that your behavior influences, in aggregate with other behaviors, and over time.[18]

In other words, while the macro environment in which your company functions and in which you and your colleagues work is to a great extent beyond your control, your workplace is not beyond your influence. The advice in this chapter can help you create the changes you want to see in yourself in the medium term to give you the best chance of improving your workplace interactions.[19] The previous chapter should help you prepare for a conversation with a colleague tomorrow and a meeting next week; this chapter should help you do what you can over time to be in a different situation six months or a year from now.

In order to improve your chances of positive workplace interactions down the road, and for those more positive interactions

---

18. A good expression of this approach to leveraging micro interactions toward broader changes is the chapter "Leveraging Small Wins" in Debra E. Meyerson, *Rocking the Boat: How to Effect Change Without Making Trouble* (Boston: Harvard Business Review Press, 2008), 101–20.

19. For an interesting look at the possible impact of small changes, see "The Ministry of Nudges," Katrin Bennhold, *New York Times, Sunday Business*, December 8, 2013, 1, 4. The ongoing work on the potential impacts of small changes and interventions is popularly expressed in Richard H. Thaler and Cass R. Sunstein, *Nudge* (New York: Penguin, 2009 [rev. and exp.]).

to become the norm if they are not now, I recommend that you focus on two separate areas, one on others and one on yourself. First, learn about your company and your workplace audience in order to better understand their interactions with you. Second, work on your presentation skills and your sense of self-confidence in order to influence how your colleagues interact with you.

FOCUS ON YOUR COMPANY AND YOUR AUDIENCE WITHIN IT

By your company, I mean not just the collection of people, products, and service that make it up, but where it is in its market. Unless you are a solo entrepreneur, have a relatively senior job, or are in a company with very few employees, you most likely engage with the company business at a micro level, paying attention to your project or your group's work, and maybe to its presence in the media. It is worth your while to figure out a bit about your company's position at a macro level: What is its market share? Who are its main competitors, and how are you doing against them? What might be your company's next product, or customer? How does your company fit into the economic landscape of the town or city and state where it is located?

If you understand what your company is trying to do at a macro level, you will understand better how your current project or product fits into your company's strategy. You will grasp the rationale for strategic decisions being made, or perhaps you will not consider the decisions being made good ones, in the light of what you learn. If that is the case, you can ask why they were made. Finally, you will better understand your colleague's behavior. At some point, you will have a rough interaction with a colleague, who will, when prodded, confess that she is in a bad mood because her boss is in a bad mood. Why? This product launch is really critical, and everyone is stressed out. Why? Ah, you will realize, one of our competitors is gaining market share on us, and people are worried.

This is not just abstract knowledge, however interesting, and it is not just business knowledge, however useful. It is knowledge about how you should interact with a colleague. If you know, or realize, someone is worried about the overall direction of the business and gets grouchy with you in a meeting, you are far more likely to take her aside afterwards and say "So, what's up?" or "Tell me what's going on, and how I can help." You will know better when to let something slide and when to address something directly, and both you and your colleague will be better off.

Over time, as you learn more about the business, you will have more and more context for what is motivating your colleagues and influencing them daily. This knowledge will help you decide what to address and what to let go. Most important of all, it will help you understand which interactions are about you and your colleague and which are about something else entirely. (It will also, by the way, help you improve your business judgment and advance your career.)

As you learn more about your company, you will also get a better understanding of how you can contribute to its success. Interestingly, the more you get to know about what your business does, the more you will recognize the skills you possess that may not be required in your current job but may nonetheless be useful. You almost certainly know more than you think. Elizabeth Samet, who teaches English literature, film, and composition at West Point, wrote an article about how she teaches plebes, "at the bottom of the institutional hierarchy," many of whom are unacquainted with the military when they arrive on campus, to recognize what they know, and how to use it flexibly.[20] Almost no

---

20. Elizabeth D. Samet, "Sherlock Holmes the Superhero," *The New Republic*, November 8, 2010, http://www.newrepublic.com/article/books-and-arts/78939/sherlock-holmes-the-superhero.

one is hired for everything she knows or does; the applicability of your full knowledge base and skills only becomes apparent in context. It's also worth remembering that not only is your knowledge base broader than you may recognize, but your skills are more broadly applicable than you may realize.[21]

In addition to understanding the business your company conducts, you also need to understand how your workplace functions. Workplaces are ecosystems of their own, and you should spend some time thinking about how the component parts of yours work together: your boss, your peers, the broader group of colleagues you work with, and anyone outside your company with whom you routinely interact, including customers, vendors, and service providers. You should consider how you engage with all of those different groups, and what you need and want out of each encounter.

While it is true that all of those individuals operate in the same workplace ecosystem, you, your colleagues, and your service providers all have different expectations of their workplace, some startlingly different. There's a great deal of literature out there about the different ways men and women view their workplace and their colleagues and how in turn men and women are viewed.[22] To the extent that you understand the influences on

---

21. Sandberg's example of this flexibility, a colleague at another company who called to ask her what problem Sandberg needed solved and then came on board to solve it, though it was outside her previous areas of expertise, appears at the beginning of the chapter "It's a Jungle Gym, Not a Ladder" of *Lean In* (52–63).

22. See Pat Heim, *Hardball for Women: Winning at the Game of Business* (New York: Plume, 1993, 2005), especially the chapter "We Live in Two Different Worlds" (233–38) for a discussion of the supposedly same world having different messages for and effects on boys and girls, men and women. See also the title page of each chapter of the same book for the different messages about the same topic given to boys and men than to girls and women. Here too I recommend Makoff's overview of handling humor in the workplace and understanding how different colleagues view it differently: "Humor: His and Hers" (95–107).

the group dynamics in your workplace, you will be better able to engage with them in a productive, satisfying way. You will also be better able to avoid a mental trap: unconsciously thinking that "equality" is the same as "the same." You of course want everyone in your workplace to be evaluated and rewarded by the same standards, and that is a requirement of any workplace that satisfies and engages all its employees. But even in workplaces that strive for that and achieve it, at least a lot of time, men and women will very often not behave the same ways.[23]

If you fall into the trap of thinking equality is the same as "the same," you may also adopt its oversimplifying engagement strategy: you should treat everyone alike. It sounds good in a way, and, in regards to professional courtesy, the workplace-inflected version of the Golden Rule, it's a no-brainer. When it comes to specific workplace interactions, however, it's more complicated. In thinking about the various ways you approach different people in your workplace, consider this exercise I used when I taught expository writing. You have been given a family heirloom watch as a graduation gift, but you lose the watch the first time you wear it. Write one e-mail explaining this loss to your grandmother, who gave you the watch, another to your mother, and one to your best friend. You will undoubtedly address each person differently, because each has a different relation to you, wants something different out of the interaction, and has a different context for it. You should apply similar principles to your workplace interactions.

The less someone interacts with you on a daily basis, the less familiar that person is with your behavior in the workplace. As a result, it's the people with whom you interact least frequently who will more often react to you on the basis of your immediate behavior (what they see right then) rather than your overall work

---

23. That is Heim's and Makoff's point. In a less benign way, that is also Virginia Valian's point in chapter 7, "Evaluating Women and Men," of *Why So Slow? The Advancement of Women* (Cambridge, MA: MIT Press, 1999).

(which they don't know much about). So your boss's boss might see you and a colleague disagreeing sharply in a meeting and wonder if you both are okay with each other, whereas your boss, who sees this frequently and knows these kinds of interactions help you get to the right answers, doesn't give it a second thought. Your boss's boss might wonder if you can be safely entrusted with a customer presentation, given how sharply you spoke to your colleague, whereas your boss is fine with it, knowing that you will not speak that way to a customer.

What you want to be aware of is not only how you are interacting with your colleagues, but how you appear to others who aren't familiar with you or your work. You should understand your workplace dynamics so that you present yourself appropriately to whoever is interacting with you or watching an interaction. That means they have enough context at hand to make an informed judgment about your knowledge of your subject, your execution in your current role, and your collegiality. For you, that means knowing whom you are dealing with, what roles they have at the company, and what they need from your interactions with them.

Over time, the knowledge of your company, its business, and your workplace dynamics will become second nature to you, and it won't be something you focus on observing and learning about on a daily basis. It will provide you with the context for interactions so you can better choose whether, when, and how to engage with your colleagues.

FOCUS ON YOURSELF

The company in its marketplace and your audience in the workplace are, for the most part, examples of things outside your control. On a day-to-day basis you don't have much influence over your company's position in the marketplace and on your workplace's functioning. You can and should learn about them, however, and understand the impact they are having. You do have more influence over your own behavior and position, and how that behavior influences your position in your workplace over time.

You must, of course, be in command of your material: you have to know what your job entails, know what parts of it you currently know how to do, and have a plan to learn the rest, whether that is a short-term plan (figure out the Excel formula in time to compute your data for a presentation tomorrow) or a long-term plan (apply for your next training course to advance your knowledge and skills). I assume you are in command of your material; the rest of this section concerns how you present it and thereby present yourself.

Some things about you that influence how you are received at work you cannot change: your height, your gender, where you went to school, the pitch of your voice, and so on. You can, however, influence how those things are perceived. In addition, some aspects of your workplace presence do respond to training. The single most important and influential of these trainable skills is presentation, everything from large-scale presentations to Q&A sessions to one-on-one conversations. Out of stronger presentation skills comes stronger self-confidence.

Presentation anxiety is common, so common that an entire organization has sprung up to give people practice at public speaking. It's called Toastmasters, and a lot of people have found it a helpful, inexpensive way to develop presentation skills and address anxiety about speaking in public. It is also useful in two other key ways: first, most chapters are organized outside workplaces, so you will find that their meetings have people from many different kinds of workplaces and fields. It's often an advantage to be able to learn this skill away from your work colleagues, and there's nothing like people with fresh perspectives to give you new advice. You will meet a range of people at different stages of their work lives, and many of them will have very good advice. Second, it's an excellent networking venue, for many of the same reasons: lots of new people from many different fields. You can find the organization at www.toastmasters.org.

If the pitch of your voice concerns you, and if presentation training doesn't address it to your satisfaction, you may want to consider some kind of voice coaching. Voice coaching can range from what you learn as a member of a singing group to the skills you gain from a community acting group, where you learn to project your voice, adapt it to your character's part in the play, and change it as action requires. You can also get individual voice coaching from a variety of sources. In general, it's better to start working on presentation skills first, and then take on additional voice coaching only if needed, as voice issues (anxiety-induced squeaks, high pitch from tension, or a tendency to speak too low to be heard) are more often symptoms of presentation anxiety than causes in and of themselves.

A recent popular development in presentation training and group interaction is improv. Improv training has been developed for and by professional actors and comics, who depend on these skills for their living. It has proved so useful that it has now been extended to many other professions, especially law. Improv training forces you into direct, close contact with an audience and teaches productive engagement skills. Critically, it puts you into situations where you are not in control: you go in with some material, but your audience may not respond, or may not respond appreciatively, and you might be heckled.[24] It also teaches you how to adapt and improvise in response to the audience's input.

---

24. Daniel Weiss, "Memo to science nerds: learn improv," *Al Jazeera America*, March 15, 2014, http://america.aljazeera.com/articles/2014/3/15/memo-to-science-nerdslearnimprov.html, and Kelly Wrather, "8 Content Marketing Lessons From Improv," *Search Engine Watch*, March 3, 2014, http://searchenginewatch.com/article/2331741/8-Content-Marketing-Lessons-From-Improv.

Given how much most workplaces require collaboration, or at the very least cooperation, and how often that collaboration takes place in meetings and presentations, you can see why this training can be useful.

If you are getting ready for a presentation coming up sooner than will be helped by skills acquired from, say, joining Toastmasters or starting an improv class, a short-term exercise involves just you and one other person. Give the presentation for your friend or colleague, and have him or her give you feedback. Better still, have him or her record you, even with something as simple as a smartphone video camera, and review it. Pay particular attention to how fast you speak, how fast your eyes move from point to point, and what you do with your hands. I have been giving public presentations to groups of various sizes for more than thirty years, and I learn something new every time I do this exercise.

Over time, stronger presentation skills will help you develop and maintain greater self-confidence. Presentation skills and self-confidence exist in a self-perpetuating, self-reinforcing cycle: if you give a good presentation, or lead a good meeting and discussion, your confidence grows, even though you are probably in no better command of your material than you were before that single meeting an hour ago. If you are self-confident, your presentations and your meetings tend to go better, even though your self-confidence doesn't in and of itself speak to your command over your material.

As you get to know your company, its business, and your workplace dynamics, your confidence in interacting with your colleagues will grow. In the case of the problematic interactions I discussed, as you find out which responses work, you will get more confident about your own engagement tactics. Here too the single most useful thing you can do to improve your presentation skills, both how well you do at them and how you feel about how well you do, is to practice. There's a good reason role-playing is so often a feature of training: it helps.

TEN WORKPLACE COMMANDMENTS

So, you've gotten better at handling tactical workplace interactions. And you've started developing the longer-term skills that, over time, will help you improve how you present your work and gain confidence as you do. Where do you land? With luck, you are better positioned in your current job, where you may stay a long time. But bearing in mind the statistics about how often people change jobs these days,[25] it's worth considering how the tactics you improve and the longer-term skills you develop can not only help you in your current job but also get you ready for your next one. The good news is that what you need to do to succeed and be more comfortable in your current job also prepares you for your next job. Here are ten workplace commandments to help you think about what kind of colleague you would like to be, how you can improve or maintain good relations with your colleagues, and what you can do to help yourself in your current job and advance your career. You'll also find a few "don'ts," or anti-commandments if you like, flipping the advice on its head to warn you away from its excesses or misuses.

1. *Value collegiality.* Be and be known as a good colleague. Collegiality is different from friendship, though it may of course include friendship. Most important, it covers how

---

25. The Bureau of Labor Statistics issued a report on the number of jobs (11.3) held by the youngest baby boomers, born 1957–1964, and it shows that workers of this generation changed jobs much more frequently than you would think, even discounting early-in-life lower-wage jobs: http://www.bls.gov/news.release/pdf/nlsoy.pdf.

you treat your colleagues who are not your friends and helps address the old offensive canard that men have colleagues and women have friends. Treat everyone with professional courtesy, including the people who have less prominent roles than you may have now: parking-garage attendants, cafeteria staff, janitorial staff, everybody. Treat everyone as someone on whom your success partly depends, because it does. Treat everyone as someone who might either be your boss or work for you someday, because that might happen. Treat everyone as someone who might give you a tip about a job, mention you to his or her current boss, give you a tip about a new customer or line of business, or help you with a problem. Being a good colleague doesn't mean you never disagree with others. Indeed, disagreement, thoughtfully done, is a high compliment: you're saying someone's ideas are worth engaging with and worth making better. Don't be seduced by the short-term ease of always being thought "nice."[26] Don't be a good colleague only to those perceived as having power.

2. *Help others.* When colleagues need help, answer their questions: help them with an Excel formula, tell them what the executives or your boss particularly hates to see in presentations, tell them what your last engagement with a particular customer was like, tell them your four favorite interview questions. If you can't help right then, tell them when you can get back to them, and then get back to them by that time. This doesn't mean you take on someone's grunt work, or their job. Don't routinely accept work or

---

26. For an interesting look at a mother who doesn't want to socialize her daughter to be nice, see Catherine Newman, "I do not want my daughter to be 'nice,'" *The New York Times*, July 31, 2013, http://parenting.blogs.nytimes.com/2013/07/31/i-do-not-want-my-daughter-to-be-nice/. For the strongly divisive reactions to this position, read the comments.

tasks that aren't your own, but do stay late to help a team in a pinch or go get a client while your colleague is struggling to load the presentation. Just be clear with your colleagues what your job is and is not.

3. *Thank people who help you.* Thanking people is a simple thing, and you would be surprised how often it is not done. I don't mean formal recognition after a big project, or a gift certificate for someone who has put in a lot of extra hours, though those things are good to do and welcome by the recipients. I mean saying "Thanks for the help!" when you receive the kind of help I encourage you to give your colleagues. Thank someone at the end of a meeting: "I want to call out [colleague] for help assembling the data for the last few slides." Thank anyone who helped you with the kind of information I mentioned under "Help others" above: "Thanks! That made the Excel SO much easier for me." Send a quick e-mail to someone's boss and say "Wow, [colleague] was so helpful with that presentation to the customer." Don't say thank you only to your superiors, or when your boss can hear you, or for work perceived as important, or as it gets closer to performance-management time.

4. *Keep a work diary.* Nearly every one of my women colleagues has underestimated the amount of work she has done, and as a result has not gotten credit for it when it comes time for performance reviews, salary increases, bonuses, and just plain understanding of the scope of her work. The simple way to avoid this classic problem is to keep a work diary. A work diary needn't be elaborate or time consuming. Put a recurring meeting on your calendar at the end of every week to write a short summary of what you accomplished that week (two or three phrases is fine),

what new work or projects you started, what new skill or information you learned, whom you helped, and whom you thanked. The last two points serve a dual function—they remind you to say thank you, and, when it comes time for performance evaluation and peer feedback, they indicate whom you should ask. Pro tip: don't plan to do this on Mondays, when the blizzard of new work and memories of the weekend will obliterate memories of the previous workweek. Bonus: if you do this every week, writing your part of your performance evaluation is infinitely easier.

5. *Find other colleagues whose judgment you trust.* Seek out the people who give good feedback in meetings, who have been in your job and been promoted, and who have reputations as good managers and good individual contributors. Seek out people whom you believe are smarter than you, and who intimidate you. Identify the most senior women in the organization and consider which are good role models, and why. Ask them to join you for coffee or lunch, tell them what you observed and admired, and ask their advice about your company (for advice about your *career*, see "Find a mentor" below). Identify colleagues whom you actively do not want to emulate, and articulate why. "Because [colleague] is a total jerk" does not count as articulating a reason; "Because [colleague] puts down people's work behind their back and then takes credit for their work" does.

6. *Find a mentor.* A mentor should help guide your career development, as well as offer advice and examples about how to handle current work challenges, what you might do next, and how you might develop your skills.

Consider finding one at your workplace and one outside your workplace, and think about finding one male and one female mentor. It is more important to find one that you trust than one who fits any particular one of these categories, however. A mentor should help you step back, assess the wider workplace landscape, and help you consider how to get there. A mentor doesn't, however, help you with your daily workload or interactions, or go to your boss or difficult colleagues on your behalf.[27]

7. **Cut yourself some slack when you aren't perfect, or the day isn't perfect.** When the kinds of interactions I've discussed happen to you at work, it's at best distracting from your job and at worst depressing. And when they repeat themselves over time, despite your best efforts to make them stop, alter them, or make them easier to ignore, it's hard not to feel discouraged with your work situation, or discouraged with yourself, as though you were responsible. You are responsible for engaging with your colleagues in a professional, constructive way, and that will often mean tough interactions, some of which will not improve, or will only improve slowly. You are not responsible for changing your colleagues, and, what's more, you can't—only they can. Cutting yourself some slack isn't an excuse to be disengaged from your workplace while you are there. You owe your employer your best efforts while you are at work. If you find

---

[27]. For a good discussion of the importance of finding a mentor, and for the differences in how men and women approach this process, see the chapter "Are You My Mentor?" in *Lean In*, 64–76, especially this cautionary note: "The men wanted answers and the women wanted permission and help. . . . Now young women are told if they can just find the right mentor, they will be pushed up the ladder and whisked away to the corner office to live happily ever after. Once again, we are teaching women to be too dependent on others." (66)

you don't like your job, or your colleagues, or your field, make yourself ready to leave.[28]

8. *Read.* The broader your understanding of your job, your company, and your business climate, the better your judgment will be and the better an employee you will be. Read about your profession, its challenges, and its upcoming changes. Read about the dynamics of your generation in the workplace. Read about how the workplace is changing. Read about how the economy is affecting your company, your product line, your market, your town, and your state. Read books, e-books, blogs, social media, newspapers, and magazines. Read about social interactions.[29] One of the best ways to learn from more senior colleagues in your workplace is to ask them what they are reading. You should certainly ask your mentor what he or she recommends you read, and what books have most influenced him or her. Don't bury yourself in the theoretical so much that you disengage from your colleagues, though. And don't prowl the internet so much at your workplace that you get distracted from your actual job.

9. *Make yourself professionally ready for your next job.* When the perfect next job or next boss comes along, at your current workplace or elsewhere, make sure you can show that you are a good candidate for it. Keep your résumé

---

28. See the excellent chapter "Facing the Difficulties (and Conditions That Ease the Difficulties)" in Meyerson, *Rocking the Boat*, 141–64, for an extended discussion of balancing engagement, disengagement, and self-protective distancing.

29. You might be surprised how often workplace questions come up in advice columnists' work, and how applicable their advice on communication is to workplaces. The best of these columnists, in my view, is Carolyn Hax, whose work is widely syndicated.

current, and keep your LinkedIn profile up to date with your current résumé. If you don't have a LinkedIn profile, create one. Read LinkedIn entries of people you respect and mimic them where appropriate. Carry business cards if that is the norm in your workplace for your job level. If that is not the norm, consider creating your own business cards, with your name, e-mail address, cell phone number, and a one-line description of your work: organic root vegetable farming; mechanical engineer; law enforcement officer. Have a non-jokey home e-mail address, and don't use your work address for engagement with any other job opportunities, except for an initial contact from a recruiter. If your job requires it, have a portfolio of your most current work available for forwarding, to the extent that your work is not confidential and is shareable. Have something clean and appropriate to wear to an interview. One caveat: if you let everyone know you're destined for better and bigger things, and let them know you are always looking for those things, it might sound to your colleagues as though you are trying to escape both them and your current job. If you are, that is fine; you just have to be discreet and polite about it at your workplace.

10. *Join your professional organization(s).* You probably have several available to you: a national one for either your job or your field, and possibly a regional subgroup. In addition, local groups often cut across company and job boundaries: there may be a local women in tech or women in business group. If you are a solo entrepreneur, these groups are especially important for contacts, engagement, and moral support. Most don't cost too much to join, and some have lower rates for people in early career stages, new members, or those earning low wages. National organizations you

may be eligible to join, like the American Association of University Women or a veterans' organization, may also be useful to you. If you find yourself paying more attention to your sponsoring organizations than to your workplace, it's a sign that you may want to look for a different kind of job than the one you now have.

Life Outside of Work

SOMETIMES IT'S HARD TO FOCUS at home because work is difficult or distracting, and sometimes the reverse is true. It's not possible to manage either work or home life so that neither ever intrudes on the other, and having that as a goal will only make you crazy. There are some areas, however, where basic planning can help make sure that your daily home life does not unduly intrude on your work. The advice in this section is meant to help you think about the large-scale issues that, once addressed, give you the peace of mind and confidence to focus on the day-to-day details of your workplace.

FINANCES

You need to understand your finances: where you stand currently, what you want to do with your money, and what you need to do to get there. In the context of this book, you need to do it so you can make good decisions at work with a realistic understanding of whether and how your finances constrain your decisions.

Not understanding your finances can cause creeping anxiety from not knowing answers to basic questions: Can I quit my job today? In six months or a year? Ever? Can I afford to take a pay cut to try that cool new job I saw listed? The good news is that these questions have data-driven answers that are based on information you have, rather than these kinds of answers: "Who knows?" or "Probably never, with my luck." Once you have fact-based answers, you can make informed decisions, minimize bad surprises, and perhaps even receive good ones.

Anxiety stemming from being financially uninformed can certainly spill over into your time at work. Indeed, when you're anxious about your finances, it can be hard to concentrate on anything else. But there can also be more direct consequences: not having a good understanding of your finances and what flexibility you do and do not have can lead you to make fundamental mistakes about your job. Let's say you're unhappy at work, but you push those thoughts away because you think you can't quit. The reality, however, may be that with a little planning, you could leave in a year and have some financial cushion to hunt for another job. You'd probably have a better attitude and be happier if you knew that, don't you think? Or if you found out it would be hard for you to leave anytime soon, you might seek help from HR, a company training program, or a friend. Either way, you're better off than you were before you had a handle on your financial state.

Thinking you're more flexible than you really are can be as bad as not knowing at all. Say you're angry about something at work, but because you think you can quit and be financially all right, you take out your anger on your colleagues instead of resolving the issue in a more professional way, not caring that you are risking your job. Suddenly you're out of a job, but it is much harder to get by financially than you had thought. Or you belatedly realize you can't quit right now, but you have already made your situation at work harder than it was, and now you feel even more stuck.

To free yourself to make realistic, informed decisions at work, never mind get any sleep at night, you need to understand your finances. The two titles I recommend as good starting points, among the many available, are *Smart Women Finish Rich: 9 Steps to Achieving Financial Security and Funding your Dreams*, by Richard Bach, and *All Your Worth: The Ultimate Lifetime Money Plan*, by Elizabeth Warren and Amelia Warren Tyagi. These are excellent, inexpensive, basic guides to understanding your money and how to manage it.

Once you have a handle on the basics, you can make decisions about whether you need, want, or can afford a dedicated financial planner, financial-planning software, an accountant, or some combination of those things. Many of the tools these and other guides recommend are free or inexpensive. You don't have to become a financial planner, and this effort doesn't need to take over your life. You just have to know where you are and where you need to go, and have a realistic plan to get there.

HEALTH INSURANCE

Everyone's health history and family situation differs, but one thing that applies to every one of my readers is this: you have to have health insurance. In the United States, not having health insurance means risking bankruptcy from even a relatively straightforward injury (say, a fractured ankle from a cycling accident) and it means catastrophe from a longer-term illness. In a groundbreaking study on 2007 bankruptcies, the authors found that nearly two-thirds of all bankruptcies were related to medical issues; in 2013, an analysis relying on that study predicted similar results for the full year 2013.[30]

---

30. "Medical Bankruptcy in the United States, 2007: Results of a National Study," *The American Journal of Medicine*, http://www.pnhp.org/new_bankruptcy_study/Bankruptcy-2009.pdf. The analysis predicting similar results for 2013: Christina LaMontagne, "NerdWallet Heath finds Medical Bankruptcy accounts for majority of personal bankruptcies," *NerdWallet*, March 26, 2014, http://www.nerdwallet.com/blog/health/2013/06/19/nerdwallet-health-study-estimates-56-million-americans-65-struggle-medical-bills-2013/.

On the positive side, under the provisions of the Affordable Care Act, some things that you may have had to pay for previously are now either free or much less expensive, including many kinds of preventive care. In addition, having health care can free you to take advantage of opportunities. If you have health care, it's easier to imagine taking time away from your job, or even leaving it, to start your own business, write a book, take a training course for a new career, or take care of a spouse or child or an aging or sick relative. Those things might not be financially possible even with health care, but without it they are much, much riskier for your family finances and allow you no peace of mind. Having health insurance is a must.

It's worth remembering that the source of your health insurance will change over the course of your working life. You will "age out" of your parents' coverage[31], if you are on it; your parent or spouse might lose the job that provides coverage; you may lose or change jobs or careers. All those things happen frequently, and when they happen to you, you will need to replace the healthcare coverage you lose.

If your or your spouse's employer or your parents' plan provides health insurance for which you are eligible and which you can afford, great! If you don't have insurance at work and are not covered by someone else's plan, go to www.healthcare.gov and start exploring your options. If you have a low income, you may qualify for help with the cost of your insurance.

You absolutely must have health insurance, and there are more ways to find it affordably than ever before. If you do not now have health insurance, getting covered needs to be your first order of business.

---

31. As of this writing, children may stay on their parents' health insurance until they are 26 years old, under the rules of the Affordable Care Act of 2010.

SOCIAL MEDIA

There's a good deal of debate going on in the United States right now about how much employers should care about their employees' social media presence. As of the time of this writing (April 2014), some states are contemplating legislation that would make it illegal for potential employers to ask for your Facebook password, for example. This is one of those areas where what is legal, what seems morally right to you, and your workplace reality may differ. Some employers care about your social media presence, others only care if it comes to their attention in a bad way, and others don't care at all.

If you do not mention your job, your workplace, or your colleagues on social media such as Facebook, Twitter, Pinterest, and Instagram, your employer is much less likely to care about your social media presence than if you do. If you mention your workplace in a positive way ("My group just finished this cool new project!"), your employer may not object, but you should make sure beforehand that whoever is in charge of your company's public presence approves of your post. It may be, for example, that your customer doesn't want your project made public, or not yet, or wants to be in charge of how it is described. You will almost certainly be allowed to post company job openings. In some cases, you will be required to get anything you post about your company on social media approved beforehand; in some cases, you may not be allowed to post about your company at all, either good or bad. When in doubt, ask your HR representative or your boss.

If you mention your workplace in a negative way—let's say you lose your job in a layoff and you vent about it on Facebook or Twitter—you should be prepared for a negative reaction from your employer, and, worse, possibly from a potential future employer.

People use social media for many things, but when it comes to mentioning your workplace, the old rule "if you don't have anything nice to say, don't say anything at all" remains useful.

A gray area is when you post about yourself in a way that your employer believes reflects badly on your workplace or on your judgment. If you work for a religious institution whose principles forbid alcohol, for example, and you post photos of your multi-margarita Mexico vacation, your employer may not like it. It may be none of your employer's business, but that might not matter. The important thing for you is to understand what the explicit and implicit norms at your workplace are, and, if you violate them, to understand what the consequences may be.

Whether to socialize with colleagues online is another gray area that depends mostly on your judgment. If your company has a policy or normative behavior, follow it. If it does not have a policy, then you can invite and accept colleagues as Facebook friends, for example, at your discretion, whether they are otherwise friends or not. Be aware that the more people at work who are connected to you on social media, the more people at work who are likely to see or learn about items someone may dislike.

IF YOU HAVE KIDS

If you have kids, you need to record your wishes for their guardianship should you and any other parent or guardian die while they are still minors. There are other things to consider, such as life insurance, but guardianship is the bare minimum. An excellent free site is www.getyourshittogether.org. It is run by a woman whose husband died suddenly when she had two young kids and who was shocked by what she and her husband had left undone. It has free templates and checklists and is easy to use.

If it's uncomfortable to think about this issue, imagine how much worse it would be to have your kids wind up with someone you would not have chosen, had you expressed your wishes and made advance arrangements that met your approval. Talking to friends or colleagues with kids who have made similar arrangements can give you ideas and contacts to help you get this done. If you have a spouse, he or she may also have friends and colleagues who can recommend sources of help. Doing this need not be expensive or time-consuming, but it does need to be done.

Once you put those protections in place, you need to tell other family members about them. Particularly if you believe your choice of guardians might cause dissent in your family, it's critical to start that conversation now so that if the worst happens, your designated guardians aren't fighting with the rest of your family.

IF YOU DON'T HAVE KIDS, BUT YOU MIGHT HAVE KIDS

Whether or not to have kids is one of the two or three most consequential decisions you will make for your working life, never mind for your life outside of work. It is too personal a decision to take any single person's advice as gospel, but if you are considering having kids and you are now employed, you should consult as many women as you can who have had kids while they were working. If possible, find some women who have had kids while at your workplace. Talk to some who have returned to work and some who have not, if there are any. Your situation will differ from theirs in ways large and small, but the broader the range of their experiences you learn about, the better informed your decision will be. It's not that these conversations will or should change your decision about whether to have kids, but they may help you plan, whatever you decide.

The best short essays I have read on this topic are the two chapters "Why You Should Have Children" and "Why You Shouldn't

Have Children" in *How to Be a Woman*, by Caitlin Moran.[32] They are brief and, by themselves, not nearly enough information for any woman considering having kids, but they will start you thinking. An excellent book about parenthood (what it means to you to be a parent, rather than how to do various parenting tasks) is *All Joy and No Fun: The Paradox of Modern Parenthood* by Jennifer Senior.

Your HR department, if you are in a company that has one, will have a list of policies about parental leave, if any, and available insurance coverage, if any. In a larger firm that provides access to an Employee Assistance Program, you may be able to find information and guidance for potential or expecting parents. It is important, however, to be aware of the distance between policies and reality. You may find, for example, that while your company provides a set number of weeks of parental leave, your boss was unhappy with the last person who took that much time, and this came across in her subsequent performance reviews. Or your boss believes that women who get pregnant never do return to the paycheck workforce, so the last woman in the group who got pregnant had a training course canceled because it was not worth the investment for someone who the boss thought probably wasn't coming back. There is often a difference between what is legal, what is right, and what actually happens, and you need to know as much up front as you can.

It is worth noting the sometimes sharp divisions at work between employees who have kids and those who don't. Employees without children may resent being asked to do more at work to make up for those on maternity leave, those who leave early for a child-related appointment, or those who call in suddenly when a child is sick. If their workplace has parental-leave benefits but

---

32. Caitlin Moran, *How to Be a Woman* (New York: Harper, 2011), 211–27 and 229–39.

LIFE OUTSIDE OF WORK

doesn't apply them to family more broadly, they may resent not being able to take comparable time off to take care of a parent or relative. Employees with children, on the other hand, may resent the perception that their leaving early loads work onto their colleagues when in fact they are getting their work done before they leave for that parent-teacher conference. These dynamics may or may not appear at your workplace, but it is worth bearing them in mind when you ask people about their experience with having children while working.

It's also good to note that how you are viewed may change radically if you have children. You may be startled by the speed at which you move from being "Director of Expensive, Important Project" to "So-and-so's mom" even within your workplace. Again, this common experience should not change your decision, just inform it.

Finally, you may run into a spectacularly unhelpful, unsympathetic reaction from women who did not have any parental leave or other benefits at all available to them in their childbearing years: "I didn't have any of that. You're lucky to have anything! Stop complaining!" That may be true, and it is rarely meant with any malice at all, but it isn't helpful either. That attitude is, however, out there, and it is one more piece of information that you should be aware of.

If you are considering having kids and haven't yet gotten a handle on your finances, now is the time to start.

Why Do We Still Need This Book?

AS I WAS WRITING, I was occasionally asked why a book like this is necessary in 2014, with so much tangible, visible progress for women in the workforce, everywhere from the US Senate to the US armed forces. Surely, they say, we're beyond the need for this kind of book.

That question most often comes from my male colleagues, but sometimes from women, too. Generally the latter are either women relatively far along in their careers or at the very beginning. The older women recall those times when workplaces were much more difficult for women than they are now, with many jobs not open to women at all. If senior women judge their junior colleagues' situations by that standard, they might reasonably think the junior women are better off now than they themselves were many years ago. These women also often hold higher-ranking jobs and sometimes forget that co-workers do not say the same things around senior employees that they do around more junior ones. Judging their junior colleagues' current experience by their own may lead them to undue optimism. More experienced women have also had time to learn and refine their own responses to the kind of situations I address, and to grow more comfortable with such situations and their own responses. Some forget what it's like to be shocked by what a colleague says to you, to be at a loss for words, to be unsure about what you may and may not say, and to be frustrated with yourself for being unsure and silent. Frankly, those interactions are often ones we would all like to forget, which makes it more likely that we will.

Women at the beginning of their careers also often wonder why this book is necessary, though for different reasons. Their understanding of the workplace is often much more theoretical than practical. They arrive at their jobs having been educated about the changes in the workforce over the past forty or fifty years, and they expect to see that progress reflected at their own workplace and in others. Like more senior women, they may believe that difficult or inappropriate incidents belong to an earlier, now-departed era in the workplace, and when they begin their careers and encounter them, they are surprised and disappointed. (Employers who grumble about the expectations of young employees not matching workplace realities often miss this part of the reason, in my experience.) "I thought it would be better now" is a phrase I hear often. What exacerbated this disappointment is that younger women, especially those recently out of school or training programs, aren't always used to environments where most things are accomplished as teams, and may not be aware of how much of their job depends on interaction with their colleagues. So when they have trouble with daily interactions, it affects a much bigger proportion of their job than they may have expected, and when that part of their job is hard, the whole job is hard, to their unpleasant surprise.

This disconnect between the high-level, long-term, visible progress and the ongoing need to help women stems in part from how we perceive workplaces, which is, naturally, as outsiders. Except for our own workplaces, we are limited by the level of detail we are offered through friends, family members, and various media, which is to say, not much. We read online that women are now admitted to the combat branches of the military, but we don't see the daily working life of the young sergeant or second lieutenant who is one of the first women in her infantry brigade, struggling for acceptance. We see that women now hold twenty Senate seats, but we do not have insight into the daily reality of the young intern in a Senate office, struggling to get her memo taken seriously by a senior staffer. As a result, we tend to over-value the big picture, because that is what we are most often shown, and to under-value the daily multitudes of small experiences that make up a work environment, because we do not often see them or hear about them. The big-picture view can both reassure us about broad-scale social changes and be entirely irrelevant to an individual woman early in her career.[33]

This disjunction between the progress we see, and therefore believe in and value, and the daily grind that may be much less

---

33. Interestingly, perceptions of progress are at odds with many of the data on women's status in the workplace. The pay gap is remarkably persistent: women working full time earn $0.77 for every dollar a man earns. See the American Association of University Women's summary and downloadable report on the issue, which also links to an overview by state and congressional district: "The Simple Truth About the Gender Pay Gap," AAUW, March 10, 2014: http://www.aauw.org/research/the-simple-truth-about-the-gender-pay-gap/. 2020 Women on Boards, a national campaign to increase the percentage of women in corporate boards to 20% by the year 2020, reports that for the Fortune 1000, women directors currently represent only 16.6%, or about one in six, of all board members. You can find their report, "2011–2013 Progress of Women Corporate Directors by State, Sector, and Size of Company," at http://www.2020wob.com/sites/default/files/2020GDI-2013Report.pdf. An excellent account of the many reasons for slow progress is Virginia Valian, *Why So Slow: The Advancement of Women*. An article from *Yale Alumni Magazine* discusses the reason for the relatively slow progression of tenured women in the STEM (science, technology, engineering, mathematics) fields, examining the career of Meg Urry, astrophysicist and president-elect of the American Astronomical Society: Richard Panek, "Astronomy and gender politics," *Yale Alumni Magazine*, 57 (4) 32–39 https://www.yalealumnimagazine.com/articles/3843.

encouraging (not to mention much less uplifting to hear about) contributes to a singularly annoying workplace experience: not being believed that your situation could really be that bad, because look at all the progress! That kind of reaction can make it even harder to figure out how to proceed. You start out not being believed, and you are measuring your daily reality against what, in many ways, looks like progress and is progress. It's just not progress for you, or not right now. You have to engage on two fronts: with the behavior you are trying to address, and with the disbelief that behavior exists, or is really that bad.

When younger women hear that the workplace is better but don't feel it is better in their individual cases, they are correct, and we need to help them.

A SPECIAL NOTE FOR MEN

Many of my male colleagues have asked me what they can do to help their female colleagues. As with so many of the things I have written about here, the answers are simple, if not easy, in the workplaces where we now operate.

The very first thing men can do is believe women when they come to them with a question, comment, or concern in the workplace. I have had many well-intentioned colleagues start off by doubting that a problem or a situation brought to them by a woman could be true, or important, or difficult to handle, or even that it occurred as the woman reported it. When your first response to a woman who brings a problem with a colleague to you is "Oh, come, on, I doubt he meant that," you are giving greater validity to someone else over the woman who has entrusted you enough to broach a hard topic or ask a question. That may be your eventual response, but it should not be your first. If the operating assumption for everyone in the workplace should be "assume good intentions," the analogous assumption in this case should be "assume truthfulness and accuracy." Start by assuming the woman talking to you is not only well-intentioned but as credible as her male colleagues.

The second thing men can do is bring an open mind to their workplaces. It is possible, probable, even, that men believe they are treating everyone equally and that there is no difference in how they approach their male and female colleagues. That may be true in the case of any individual, but nonetheless a good deal of underlying data shows men and women are treated differently in the workplace, and by both men and women.[34] I urge everyone, men and women, to read *Why So Slow? The Advancement of Women* by Virginia Valian on this topic and to believe that what the data show to be broadly true may also apply to your workplace and your own interactions, and to examine yourselves and your workplace in its light.

A SPECIAL NOTE FOR MORE SENIOR WOMEN

I wrote this book for women at earlier stages of their careers, but these next few paragraphs are addressed to women further along in theirs. In a keynote speech at a 2006 luncheon celebrating the WNBA's all-decade team, Madeleine Albright remarked "[t]here is a special place in hell for women who don't help other

---

34. In a famous case of this disparate evaluation, when Cecil Bødtker's poetry was first reviewed in 1955, the reviewer assumed the poet was male and gave the work a very positive review. Later on, when her gender was known, the same reviewer wrote a much less positive review, describing the poetry as "pleasant." The incident is discussed in Toril Moi, *Sexual/Textual Politics: Feminist Literary Theory* (Methuen: London, 1985) 34–35. A more recent example appears in a discussion of the disparate prices paid for male and female artists' work: Greg Allen, "The X Factor: Is the Art Market Rational or Biased?" *New York Times*, May 1, 2005, http://www.nytimes.com/2005/05/01/arts/design/01allen.html?pagewanted=print&position=.

women."[35] For women of Albright's generation, who were often the only, or only senior, or only prominent women in their fields, the need to help other women was even greater than it is now, and perhaps more obvious. But now there is a different need: to realize that the kinds of workplaces we would all like, where everyone is valued equally for what they bring to the workplace, are not yet a reality. Younger women still need help, and we still need to give it to them.

The first thing women can do, especially women in more senior roles, is to be aware that we are role models, whether we intend to be or not. Younger women will look to senior women especially to see how we conduct ourselves at work: how we speak, act, and dress; how we treat others; how we advance in our careers; what kind of colleagues we are.[36] Depending on the kind of workplace you occupy, you may in fact be their only, or only senior, or only prominent role model.

The next thing we can do is to realize that, although younger women may have it better than we did at comparative stages of our careers, they still need help and guidance. That starts with

---

35. Mechelle Voepel, "Albright empowers all-decade team at luncheon," ESPN.com, July 13, 2006, http://sports.espn.go.com/wnba/columns/story?id=2517642. Albright was as good as her word, coaching then-candidate Elizabeth Warren on foreign policy during Warren's 2012 Senate campaign. See the discussion: Elizabeth Warren, *A Fighting Chance* (New York: Metropolitan Books, 2014), 228. In another outstanding example of women remarking on their ongoing resolve to help other women, Aine M. Brazil, a structural engineer and vice chairman at Thornton Tomasetti, describes her career at the firm and its environment for women: "'There was no glass ceiling here,' she said, 'and part of my passion is to make sure there never is one. People are always asking how I've been able to thrive in such a male-dominated profession. We don't have children, so I didn't have to balance family and career, but I'm very aware of my co-workers who do need to.'" Robin Finn, "A Shoulder for Buildings to Lean On," *New York Times, Sunday Business*, May 4, 2014, 11.

36. As just one of many examples, when you occupy a place in company leadership, how you dress will be noted, and many books of advice on workplaces advise women to emulate the dress of the senior team: see Heim, *Hardball for Women*, 124–30.

our awareness. In the introduction I mentioned a group of younger women who came to me for guidance about interactions they were having in their workplace. When I mentioned what they were encountering to some senior women of my acquaintance, they were as surprised as I had initially been, but probably none of us should have been surprised. This is my call to you to remember what it was like to be junior, if you no longer are.

Sometimes when I have talked to young women, they have said to me, "That answer might work for you, Anne, but not for us." I have had to recalibrate my advice, remembering their ages and relative experience levels and those of their peers. Senior women have had more time to get comfortable with our colleagues, and we have had more interactions to practice and get better at our own responses. The kinds of responses that work for us in our 40s, 50s, and 60s may not help young women in their 20s and 30s. Partly because we have a little more workplace experience, we might be more able than junior women to call out our male colleagues when necessary, privately and publicly if need be. And so this is also a call to remain watchful for those times when you can productively intervene, when your more junior colleagues cannot.

Lastly, if you are in a very senior role, you may find yourself in the interesting position of being pointed to as an example of how there is no longer a problem for women in the workplace. It can be flattering, but it is also incorrect.

Feedback

WHEN I BEGAN WRITING THIS BOOK, I wondered why it did not already exist. When I was about halfway through writing it, I understood much better: it's tough to enumerate the various difficult interactions that young women experience. That said, the part of writing this book that has been most helpful to me as a manager and mentor has been hearing and reading about what women are going through today. I hope you will contribute to that flow of information, if you would like, and I will revise and update subsequent editions of this book in part based on your feedback. If you would like to contact me with comments, questions, or suggestions, you can send e-mail to book-feedback@annekrook.com. I regret that, owing to the amount of e-mail I get, I am not able to answer all your questions or respond to your feedback individually, but I will answer as many as I can, and I do read everything.

If you'd like to discuss a speaking engagement for your group or workplace, please contact speaking@annekrook.com. You can see my work at my website, www.annekrook.com.

Made in the USA
Charleston, SC
21 February 2015